Praise for *Lost Teachings of the Run*

"Born out of a visceral and passionate engagement with her own northern ancestral tradition, Kincaid's book is a searching exploration of the runes and their meaning. It is a paean, a poem, a meditation, and a clarion call 'for the lost teachings of the runes to return with intensity and brilliance.' The runes spring to life with a new force as we are taken on a marvelous journey through the symbols, probing their deeper layers and many-faceted messages. For the reader who wants to work actively with the runes, this book provides a framework for orientation and a series of guided meditations. In the words of the author: 'The teachings and wisdom of the runes bring us back into harmony with all life, with our bodies and with the earth.'"

—Christopher McIntosh PhD, author of *Beyond the North Wind*

"Very impressive and emanating a great love towards the Northern heritage, and the wish to share this universally, the first part of *Lost Teachings of the Runes* is pure evocative poetry. Reading it induces a pleasant light trance from which your own ideas emerge. It's how it is written—the Dance of Runes manifesting themselves in writing. It sings! The runes are understood as primordial Living Beings,' closely entwined with nature. This is very intriguing. Containing a slew of new visualization techniques centering around The Wheel of Life, this book will appeal to Pagans of all stripes, shamanic workers, and Heathens. But it does require an open mind. This book asks many questions, well worth meditating upon. Some are very hard questions and will challenge your perceptions. Lost Teachings of the Runes is a Song of Runes. It's given me a different perspective on the runes to contemplate."

—Freya Aswynn, author of *Northern Mysteries and Magick* and *Leaves of Yggdrasil*

"The ancestors have not stopped teaching us. In *Lost Teachings of the Runes*, Ingrid Kincaid illuminates a simultaneously very new and very old way of engaging with the mystical North. The runes come alive in unique ways, embraced by a seasonal cycle and rooted in the center of the World Tree. Kincaid encourages a questioning spirit. What do you experience as the Wheel turns around? This book has answers and more questions. It is a pioneering and powerful vision."

—Dawn Work-MaKinne, PhD, and author contributor to *Goddesses in World Cultures* and *Myths Shattered and Restored*

LOST TEACHINGS OF THE RUNES

Northern Mysteries and the Wheel of Life

INGRID KINCAID

WEISER
BOOKS

This edition first published in 2019 by Weiser Books an imprint of
Red Wheel/Weiser, LLC
With offices at
65 Parker Street, Suite 7
Newburyport, MA 01950
www.redwheelweiser.com

Copyright © 2019 Ingrid Kincaid
The thirty-three rune poems were previously published in 2016 in
Runes Revealed by Inkwater Press, ISBN 978-1-62901-349-7.

ISBN: 978-1-57863-676-1

Library of Congress Cataloging-in-Publication Data available upon request.
Cover photograph © Ingrid Kincaid
Illustrations by Naomi St. Clare

Typeset in Aller Light
Printed in Canada
MAR

10 9 8 7 6 5 4 3 2 1

CONTENTS

1

The Stories   7

2

Directions of the Wheel   67

3

Using the Wheel   189

4

The Rune Beings   211

5

Guided Meditations   287

Nothing I say is true.

Everything I say is true.

The truth lives in the questions.

Life is a story.
This book is a story.
Each time you enter the story it will be different.
You will be different.
The words will be different.
Life will be different.

Life is a question.
This book is a question.
Many questions.
Changing questions.
Questions with no answers.
Questions with no right answers.

This book is alive.
This story is alive.
You are alive.

This book is a story.
Life is a story.
A story about the runes.
A story about the tree.
A story about the winds and the horizon.
A story about the ancestors.
And you, standing in the center.

Ancestors are life.
Ancestors are stories.
This book is an ancestor.
Ancestors tell us who we are.
Ancestors tell us where we come from.
And where we are going.

This book is a tool.
A useful tool.
A tool for using.
A tool for asking questions.
A tool for asking questions with no answers.

You are standing in the center.
Turning.
Asking questions.
Remembering the future.
Foretelling the past.

This book is dedicated to the stories.
This book is dedicated to the questions.
This book is dedicated to the place where you live in the story.

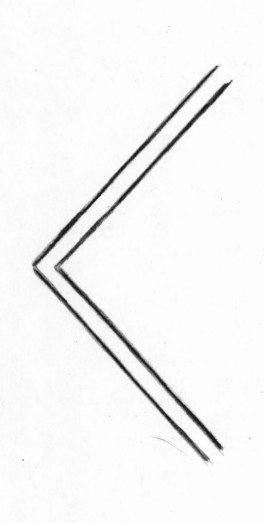

1

THE
STORIES

FINDING OUR WAY HOME

The stories we have been told are not the only stories, nor are
they the right stories.
There are other stories.
The ones that have not been told.
The ones that have been forgotten.
The ones we carry in our bones, not in our minds.
The ones our ancestors wish to tell.

It is my desire that these new stories that are actually old
stories will awaken in us something ancient.

remembering
more than blood
my ancestors
were etched inside
Kenaz
split me open
I penetrated the darkness
I saw what was destroyed
spun and woven
frayed and worn
the strands of Wyrd
retied

The earth is in upheaval, again.
Great change is upon us.
Something new is being brought into form, something that is
older than time.

Rune wisdom is reappearing for us out of the melting ice.
It is the same wisdom that fed, guided and protected our
indigenous Northern European ancestors.
It is neither female nor male.
It is neither bad nor good, dark nor light, immoral nor moral.
Rune wisdom is the wisdom of life in constant motion and
perfect balance, sourced from the darkness of the great void,
chaos coming into form and returning again to the darkness.

Sadly there are those among us who attempt to corrupt runic
wisdom with patriarchal, misogynistic, aggressive energies.
Myopic, All-Father Odinism
Neo-Nazi white supremacy
Exclusionary Asatru
Glorified Viking violence

It is time we reclaim the lost teachings of the runes, time to
remember who we are, and find our way back to our roots.

This book is about our roots.
This book is about the Center.
This book is about standing in the Center, in the present
moment, remembering who we are by connecting the future
with the past.
It speaks of ways to discover and explore what exists above,
below, beyond and inside.
It is dedicated to our bones, to our ancestors, to our stories,
told and untold, and to the questions.
It is dedicated to our journey home.

The runes have given me the strength and courage to walk away from a monotheistic, patriarchal, desert religion, the religion of the conquerors.

They have shown me the way home, back to the Motherland of Northern Europe, and my ancestral roots.

May you find your way home as well.

THE DRUM

The drum maker dreams a dream.
In his dream he is lost in the whiteout of an Arctic blizzard.
There is no direction, no horizon, no protection.
He crouches, wrapped in skins and furs.
He knows he must do something but he is afraid.
Out of the chaos of the storm, a white reindeer appears.
A snowy owl is perched on her back.
He looks away. He turns back.
The owl is an old woman.

She is playing a large drum.
The drum is marked with strange symbols.
He is certain he has never seen these symbols, yet he
remembers them.
The old woman is singing a song.
He is certain he has never heard the song, yet he knows it.
The reindeer comes so close he can feel her breath.
The old woman stops singing.
She speaks in the voice of the North Wind and the silence of
the dark and cold.
"Do not fear the powerful one. Make her the drum."
He returns from his dream. He makes the drum.

The powerful one uses her drum to remember.
She uses her drum to hear the stories that have been forgotten.
She uses her drum to listen to the ancestors.
They speak to her of the wheel.

They speak to her of the runes.
They speak to her of the lost teachings of the North.
They remind her that the past lives.
Beneath the surface of the ground on which she stands.
In the place the sun goes at the end of each day.
In the place where the dead go when they return to the earth
and the dark.
In the place where the ancestors dwell.

The drum shows her how to stand in the Center of her own life
and find the horizon. The future exists beyond the horizon no
matter which direction she turns.
The future rises up out of the past.
The runes speak to her through the drum.
They tell her that the still point in the Center is the ending and
the beginning.
The place where the World Tree grows, its roots deep, its
branches wide.
The place where we all must stand to claim our sovereignty.
She sees the runes circling around the horizon.
The horizon is the circle of sight that remembers the future.

When she drums, the ancestors come and stand with her in the
Center.
They speak to her of the realm of the dead.
The place where the sun disappears taking with it all the
shadows.
They remind her that things are hidden in the light.
They remind her that the stars can only be seen in the dark.

They teach her how to face the direction where the dark rises
up out of the earth.
They teach her how to face the direction where the light rises
up as well.
They are the same direction.
The place from which new life appears.
The place that foretells the past.

The ancestors show her the direction of the cold.
They show her the direction of the warmth.
They show her how the heavens turn above us as we watch the
stars circle in the night sky.
The ancestors speak to her through the voice of the drum
reminding her that all life is a circle, that all things continue,
that birth and growth cannot exist without death and decay and
that all things breathe, even the stones.
They remind her that the past and the future exist in the
present moment, in the Center, in the earth beneath our feet
and the horizon we can never reach.
They show her that there is no top or bottom to the earth.
It hangs in the darkness of the great void.
It too is the Center, for all space extends outward from it, no
ending, no beginning.
And the sun is the Center, and each star is the Center and each
person and each moment.
All this and more has come to pass through the drum in the
voices of the ancestors.

INHERITED GRIEF

Savage, barbaric, ignorant, uncivilized.
Primitive, crude and bloodthirsty.
These are words commonly used to describe the indigenous,
tribal people of Northern Europe.
These words are not neutral.
These words are not benign.
They are charged words, sourced from the language of the
conquerors.
Such words imply the lack of moral standards, law and order
and suggest that illiteracy is a sign of ignorance or inferiority.
For us to think of our ancestors in such a way is harmful,
disrespectful and destructive.

The Roman legions did not bring progress, nor did Christianity.
They brought change.
They brought change that was accompanied by violence,
violation and death.
Their invasions fostered disconnection from and destruction
of cultures that were deeply rooted in nature, the land, and
worship of the ancestors.

The tribal people of the Motherland of Northern Europe were
not inferior to the marching hordes of Roman soldiers.
They were different.
They had laws and standards.
They had music, art and history.
They danced and sang songs.

They were clans and tribes made up of families with children and old ones, wise and powerful women and men.
These were a people of the spoken word.
Theirs was an oral tradition.
They were storytellers who communicated in many different languages.
They knew how to speak with nature and all the unseen ones.
They were travelers, explorers, and navigators who built amazing structures that still exist, some of them older than the pyramids of Egypt.

Life was harsh for our Northern European ancestors. Many of them lived near the Arctic Circle. The winters were long and cold. The climate inspired music and poetry that reflected the deep, dark intensity of their lives.
Their spiritual culture was different from cultures in other parts of the earth.
They were not people of the desert or the Mediterranean.
They did not know the jungle or the savanna.
They were not monotheists.
They worshiped and communed with countless gods and goddesses, as well as seen and unseen beings that inhabited their land.
They did not experience these beings as mere thought-forms created by humans, nor did they call them archetypes. These beings were real and alive, present and named. They were sought for the wisdom to survive.
The indigenous Northern Europeans knew intimately the language of glaciers, the ways of the reindeer, and the glorious dance of the Northern lights in the night sky.

My ancestors come from the great Motherland of Northern Europe. My maternal grandfather was an immigrant who fled Sweden as a young man, forced by famine and disease to leave his home. Such a story is familiar to many of us with ancestors from Europe.

When I speak about the tribes of the Motherland of Old Europe I speak about my own family. They are my people. Perhaps they are your family as well. There are many of us scattered around the globe who are the progeny of these strong, courageous, resilient people of the North. Our ancestors migrated to lands all over the world. And even though we are not currently living in our ancestral homelands and perhaps have never traveled there, we still carry in our bodies, in our blood and bones, in our DNA, the memory of who we are and where we come from. It is evident in our physical appearance, our body type, our food preferences, weather preferences, our longings, and our knowing. Such memories do not disappear in just a few generations. It has only been a short time since our ancestors left their homelands.

We cannot live separate from nature. We are part of it, all of it. Our ancestors knew we could never be simply observers. Nature is in us and around us just as we are in it and around it. It speaks to us and we do well to listen. We must remember who we are and who we were before the conquerors came.

Human nature is nature.
The old stories and teachings sprang up from nature, from the geography, the terrain, the climate, the flora and fauna.

These stories are still relevant, even in this modern, digital age. There are many who live quite disconnected and removed. There are some who believe we do not need nature or that it is possible to go beyond it.

It is true that times have changed, in some parts of the world quite drastically, but we still need the same things to live, survive and continue. The past is important. We learn from the past. We are rooted in the past. We are rooted in our ancestors. These roots are what connect us to the present moment and to the future.

There is a global rekindling of interest in the runes. They are calling out to people in all parts of the earth, not just to those of us with Northern European ancestry. The runes carry wisdom that is significant and vital to human existence. They are sentient beings connected to and part of nature and the gigantic, primal forces of creation and destruction. The myths and stories woven together with the runes carry images and information that bring us back to nature and to the land, to the awe and mystery of life and death. The runes reconnect us with the lost teachings of the Northern Traditions and the indigenous, tribal folk soul of Old Europe. They are the matrix of a spiritual heritage that has been neglected and forgotten for a long time. I grieve for it. We grieve for it.

The runes are beings, older and more powerful than the gods and the giants. They are older than our human ancestors. They were there at the beginning, which is the middle of the cycle that never ends. We cannot force them or bind them nor do we need to sacrifice to them. They are indifferent to our human condition. We must listen and allow. The runes speak to us, often through vibration and resonance. They tell us when we are out of tune, out of balance, or out of harmony with nature. They did this for our ancestors as well.

We are living at a wondrous time in history.
The earth is in upheaval.
It has happened in the past, countless times, and it will continue to happen.
Endless cycles of destruction and creation.
We are in the middle of one now.
We see it all around us.
We can be afraid. We can be in awe. We cannot stop it.
The unseen ones, the giant beings of nature, are at work in ways we do not understand.
At this time when ancient wisdom, long held frozen in the ice, is being released, the ancestors are coming forward, asking and demanding to be remembered and the gods and other unseen ones and the rune beings are making their presences felt, often in very dramatic ways that cannot be ignored or pushed aside, or controlled.

Endings never happen in isolation. When something ends, something always begins.
Nothing that we face can only be about the beginning.
When something begins it has already ended.
We are birthed into death. This is what the runes teach us.
The endless cycles.
The turning of the wheel.
Circles moving within circles.

I must do this work. My ancestors and the runes called me. Perhaps an even stronger statement is, they chose me to do it. I can only speak about my own ancestors, no one else's and I cannot assume to know why someone is called by the runes or the gods or the beings of the far North. It is not for me to decide or to judge.

What I do know is that throughout my many years of sharing rune wisdom, the majority of people who come to me have strong ancestral lines that reach back to the Motherland of Old Europe, and more often than not, these lines wind their way up into circumpolar regions.

Often the people who find their way to me know little or nothing about the runes or their own ancestral, spiritual heritage. Yet they tell me they feel that the runes are somehow calling them.

They come seeking guidance, information and connection. They want to go home, to sit again at their own sacred fires. They are tired of wandering in the desert with the monotheistic Middle Eastern god.

Their throats are dry from chanting praises to Hindu deities such as Shiva, Shakti, Durga and Kali Ma.

They are like orphans who long to hear their Mother Tongue, who wish to raise the drinking horn and partake of the sacred mead of their homeland.

Where are you in this story?

GAR AND THE CIRCLE

The ancestors often visit me when it is quiet.
They show me things. I pay attention.
They tell me things. I listen.
Then I write them down.

This book grew out of such an experience.
Before it was a book, it was a class.

About ten years ago, in the middle of the night, I began to
see patterns on my bedroom ceiling. It looked as if the starry
heavens were rotating overhead. As I watched I saw Gebo
moving toward Ingwaz, the two runes coming together to
form the rune Gar. Because of the way the patterns were
rotating, I imagined a circle around Gar. The circle gave me a
way to visualize, locate and explain what I was being shown.
I called it the Circle of Life.

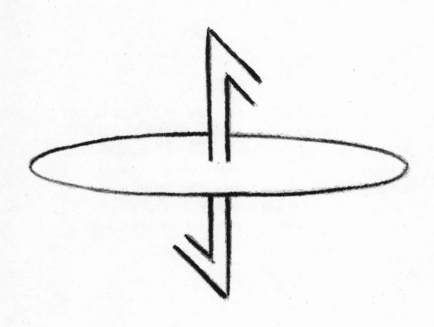

I was shown the World Tree growing in the center of Ingwaz which forms part of Gar, at the point where the arms of Gebo cross each other. The tree roots grow down below the surface. Its branches reach up toward the sky. Its trunk connects them both.

I was shown the Eihwaz rune placed in the Center, piercing through the circle, half above and half below. The Tree embodies the Eihwaz rune and the rune vibrates with the Tree. It is a rune of life and death.

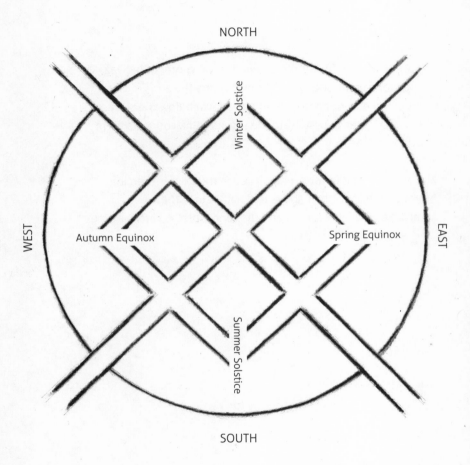

Placing the encircled Gar flat you can see it as a map and a calendar. The four points of Ingwaz align with the four compass directions, North, East, South and West.

They also mark or indicate the seasonal events of Winter Solstice, Spring Equinox, Summer Solstice and Autumn Equinox.

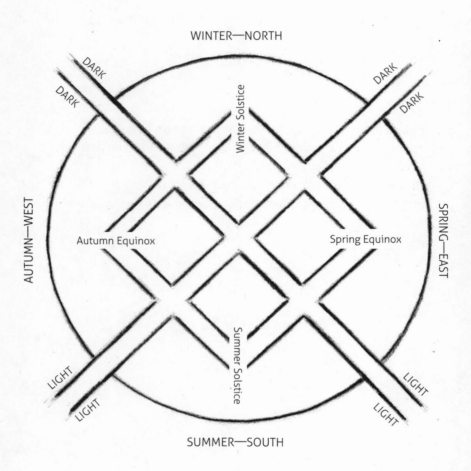

The arms of Gebo provide the beginning and ending divisions for the seasons, the halfway points between the Solstices and the Equinoxes. They correspond approximately with the dates February 1, May 1, August 1 and November 1.

The year's cycle can also be divided into two parts, the dark half and the light half.

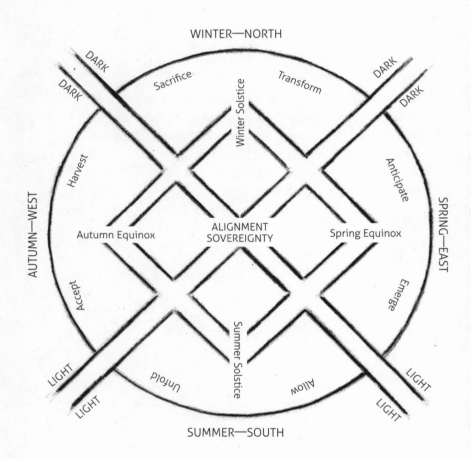

WINTER—NORTH

DARK

DARK

Sacrifice

Transform

DARK

DARK

Winter Solstice

Harvest

Anticipate

AUTUMN—WEST

SPRING—EAST

Autumn Equinox

ALIGNMENT
SOVEREIGNTY

Spring Equinox

Accept

Emerge

Summer Solstice

LIGHT

LIGHT

Unfold

Allow

LIGHT

LIGHT

SUMMER—SOUTH

The divisions created by the arms of Gebo can represent progression through life experiences.

East: Anticipate—Emerge
South: Allow—Unfold
West: Accept—Harvest
North: Sacrifice—Transform

I gathered together the wisdom and the images I had been given and I created a class. Each time I taught the class I gained more insights.
I was being drawn deeper and deeper into the Center.
The single point formed by the crossed arms of Gebo.
The place where the Tree was growing.
Something shifted and intensified once I began to write the book.
The ancestors knew I was ready.
They gave me another message,

Focus on the Center.
Teach it from the Center.
Connect with the Tree that grows in the Center.
Roots deep below the surface, beneath your feet.
Branches reaching up into the sky.
Align yourself with the trunk.
You are the Sovereign ruler of the limited sphere of influence that is your present life.
Teach it from the Center.

The message was quite clear.
I needed to remember.

The wisdom of the runes and the lost teachings are rooted in the Center and exist beyond the horizon and beneath our feet. All of this could be spoken of as the Circle of Life and yet it was so much more than a circle.

The ancestors knew I had to return to Gar and teach from the Center.

I needed to be reminded as well that Gar was the tip of the spear and the point of the distaff. It held the Center around which the runes circled.

And the Center was Sovereignty, the sovereignty of each of us as individuals.

The present stands between the past and the future and they exist beyond the horizon. They cannot be limited because the horizon is fluid. It creates an edge but we are never bound by it because the horizon moves with us as we move.

It is not a stagnant circle.

A change in location creates a shift in perspective.

A shift in perspective allows for a different experience.

For example, our horizon, our limited circle of sight, will be quite different depending on whether we are standing on a mountaintop or living in a deep and narrow valley.

How you experience life is different each day because each day is different. You cannot go to a new place and experience it through the overlay of preconceived ideas. You must ask the questions in each moment.

Who am I?
Where am I?
What time is it?
What do I need?
Which way is the wind blowing?

These five questions are like keys that unlock and open the way
for you to access the teachings of the runes.

Whenever you orient yourself in relationship with the horizon,
remember that you are always standing in the Center, with the
Tree.

How broad is your horizon?
How far can you see?
Do you feel confined within the circle?
Do you use it to know where you are?
Does it hold time for you or are you holding time with it?
Does your perspective restrict or confine your ability to relate
to the present moment and the place where you are?

The message I had received from the ancestors became even
more clear.
The wisdom is held in the shape of the rune.
When you step into the Center of Gar the circle you see is the
horizon.
The horizon is not permanent.
It is ever changing, moving, revealing, and hiding.
It is not necessary to draw it.

You have to experience the teachings from the Center,
the place where you stand, in your own sovereignty,
facing the horizon.
The focus of the class changed as I wrote this book.
I was remembering.

As you read this book and work with the teachings it is my hope
that you will come to understand and embody the practice
of standing in the Center, in your own Center, growing in
appreciation of the wisdom of the runes.

Stand in the Center of your life, no matter where you are, and
face the horizon.
Ask yourself the questions,

Who am I?
Where am I?
What time is it?
What do I need?
Which way is the wind blowing?

The answers to these questions will never be the same. They
are determined by your own perspective in the present
moment, your own personal experience, never the experience
of someone else.

Do you begin your day with the rising of the sun or the return
of the dark?
Which way do you turn to track the sun across the sky?
Do you turn to the right or to the left?

The answer is different depending on whether you live north or south of the equator or even if you live on the equator.
What kind of weather does the wind bring?
We cannot bind the winds or the weather or the movement of the heavens to a wheel.
Nor can we bind creatures or plants, colors or chants, claiming they belong to one certain direction or season.
The Circle of Life is a symbol, a tool. It represents the infinite nature of energy, the taking and giving back, the movement and changes that exist within cycles that are always the same.

Remember that the teachings of the runes come to us from the people of the North, people who intimately knew long, harsh winters when the sun barely kissed the horizon. Their growing season was short. Their summers and autumns were spent preparing for the return of darkness.

Rune wisdom is earth wisdom. Earth is our home. It was their home as well. We need rune wisdom just as they did and to benefit from it we must be able to relate it to our own personal experiences in actual time and place.

What do you see?
What do you feel?
What do you know?

The runes are not static.
They are alive.
They vibrate, pulse and shimmer.
They breathe.

They do not exist all lined up in a certain order, like an alphabet, nor are they confined in special groupings.
Humans have contrived such systems as a way to capture them, preserve them and hold them in memory.

They are not flat.
They are multi-dimensional and their lines extend out in all directions intersecting each other and in so doing they replicate themselves, forming and reforming their own shapes and the shapes of each other.

Do not try to affix the runes to the circle. They move freely around and through time and each rune holds a rightful place in each section or direction, in each season or experience. Whenever we try to capture them, we get stuck, limiting ourselves and our relationship with these primal beings.

There might be times when you see the circle around Gar and times when you do not.
If you use it in a way that restricts or confines your ability to relate to the present moment and your location, it does not serve you.
Return to the Center and remember.

THE HORIZON

We know where we are on the earth by finding the horizon. It is the place of appearing and disappearing, the edge place, the border, the apparent boundary between earth and sky. It is a circle of sight, a limiting circle. It is the limit of our visual range as well as our knowledge and perception.

You can walk toward the horizon, walk into the future as it is unfolding before you but you can never arrive. Each step you take is in the present moment. Behind you is the past. Ahead of you is the future. Or quite possibly it is the other way around. The horizon is our relationship with the rising and setting of the sun, the arrival of light and the arrival of dark.

We know movement on the earth because we move upon it.
We know movement on the earth because the heavenly bodies move above us.
We do not experience the earth itself moving, unless of course we experience an earthquake beneath our feet.
When you stand in the Center of your own life, you know where you are. You know what you need and what time it is by orienting yourself with the horizon.

Our ancestors used the horizon to know where they were, what time it was and what they needed. Such knowledge was crucial to their existence. Strong evidence of their intimacy with the horizon and the movement of the heavens is present in the ancient structures they erected. Some are still standing. Some are more than 5000 years old. The megaliths, the circles of stones, the burial cairns, these monuments are in perfect alignment with and mark events that occur on the horizon. The rising and setting of the sun and moon, as well as the stars overhead.

Is it necessary for us to know how to find the horizon?
Is it important to know where the sun rises or the moon sets?

Absolutely. The earth is our home. Imagine living in your home and not knowing where the front door is or how to find the kitchen.
Connection to the earth is vital to knowing who we are, where we are and what time it is. It is foolhardy to depend solely on modern devices and gadgets. They are dependent upon signals and electricity. They are useful and it is dangerous to assume they will always work. Learn to use your body to know where you are.

The horizon is the future and the past existing simultaneously as we stand in the present moment. It is behind us and in front of us no matter which way we turn.
As you read through this book exploring lost teachings and hidden wisdom you will see I often reference the horizon and the events that happen there. We orient ourselves in life in relationship to the circle of sight.

Turn and face the direction where the sun rises up out of the earth. We call this East, the place of the dawn. When you face the rising sun your back is turned to the direction called West, the place where the sun disappears.

If you lift your arms while facing East and hold them
outstretched from your body, your right arm will be pointing
toward the place we call South and your left arm will be
pointing North.

Walking toward the horizon or into the horizon is to move
toward something new, something that exists already but that
you have yet to see or experience. Even though things exist
outside of or beyond the circle of sight, they do exist and are
connected to you by the edge.
The sun is there beyond the horizon even before it appears.
And the darkness exists even before it fully emerges.
This is some of the wisdom held in the rune Ior.
This is some of the wisdom of the world serpent, Jormungund,
who speaks to us of borders, boundaries and edges.

The future is hidden, just beyond the horizon.
The past is hidden there as well.
There are many things hidden and concealed.
The inside of things.
The other side of things.
Underneath and below the surface.
The past lies hidden inside our bodies, the story of our heritage
and the life we have lived so far.
The past is visible on the outside as well.
The future exists inside our bodies.
The future exists outside our bodies as well.
We have the ability to create from within and we have the
ability to bring forth.
Our bodies will ultimately feed the earth so we are becoming
the future.

The future and the past exist simultaneously, both inside and outside, beneath and beyond.

There is the place beneath our feet that is hidden. It is the past held in layers of soil, sediment and stone. It is into this past below the surface that seeds and nuts and bulbs send their roots to be nourished so the future can rise up.

As we face the disappearing sun the dark rises up from the earth behind us.

Is this the future or the past, or both?

This is the wisdom of the runes.

When you remember to stand in your Center, with integrity, courage and honor, you will find yourself at home, here on the earth, in the Center of the great darkness of the void, Ginnungagap.

You will remember who you are, where you come from and realize there is no place to go.

You will claim your sovereignty as the sole ruler of your own limited sphere of influence, your own circle of sight.

You will realize your circle of sight, your horizon, touches and overlaps with the circles of all who are around you, all life, all beings.

You will know what time it is, which way the wind is blowing and come to realize exactly what you need in order to live in harmony and balance with all that is, all that was, and all that lies beyond the horizon and beneath your feet.

THE TREE

When you step into the Center, you will find the Tree.
The Tree was there in the beginning, in the yawning void,
Ginnungagap.
We know this to be true from the stories of our ancestors.
We know that the realms of Muspelheim and Niflheim were
there, in the beginning, slowly drifting back and forth.
It was also the ending.

We know that the Tree had branches and roots and that there
were Nine Worlds, possibly more, in the roots.
And the Wells were there, in the roots.
And the Nornir were there, in the roots, beside the Wells.
And the runes were there, numberless, like the stars that are
mere pinpoints of light in the great darkness of the void.

Standing in the Center connecting with the Tree, when did you
enter the story?

There are some who speak of this Tree, this ancient being, only
by the name Yggdrasil. To do so is to diminish its age and its
presence, to shrink it down to the smallness of the one god, the
so-called high god, to focus only on his sacrifice.
Yggr, perhaps meaning terrible, is one of the many names of
Odin.
Drasill meaning horse could be speaking of Odin riding the
horse as a sacrifice, perhaps suggesting that this was the
mighty tree from which he hung himself.

Using only the name Yggdrasil limits our knowing of this ancient being, the World Tree.

The Tree was there long before Odin was birthed from the body of his giantess mother, Bestla.
Long before Bestla was birthed from the body of her giantess mother.
The Tree was there in the beginning.
Roots deep.
Branches high.
Watered by Wells.
Guarded and tended by the Nornir.

What was its name in the beginning?
What was its name before Odin?
There are some who say the Tree is called the Pillar of Mimir.
This links it back to one of the Wells, Mimisbrunnr.

Remember that even though it is said that the gods gather beneath the Tree to take counsel, it is to the Well that Odin goes, seeking wisdom.
And to the giant Mimir, who is perhaps his mother's brother, his uncle.
Could it possibly be that Mimir is older than the giants?
Perhaps Mimir is someone other than we think.

There are those who speak of the Tree by another name.
Laerath, the Guardian or the Listener.
When did you enter the story?
Early on with the Norns of Fate?
Or later, with Odin?

Could it be that the memory of the Tree is preserved in the Irminsul, the holy pillar honored and revered by the Saxons? It held the sky in place, preventing it from crashing to the earth. Is it represented by the god pillars of Scandinavia, carved with faces, adorned with nails?

When we step into the Center we remember our connection with the Tree. We remember our place. The silence. The Winds. The Wells. The beginning. The ending. The equal exchange that occurs, through the trunk, between the roots in the soil beneath our feet and the branches that extend beyond the horizon. What name do you use when you speak of the Tree?

The Tree holds it all, above and below, connecting the seen and unseen.
Rising up. Sending down.
The roots that remember the future.
The branches foretelling the past.
The trunk connecting it all in the present.
The Tree provides the vantage point from which we can see the horizon, the place where things appear and disappear, the place where the light and the dark rise up out of the land and sea, as well as the place where the present disappears, becoming the past, which continuously feeds the future.

Is the Tree an ash?
Could it be a yew?
The lore speaks of this mighty Tree as being ever green.
The ash is not ever green. The yew is.
Yew is considered to be a tree connected to life and death. Its branches grow up and then curve down, rooting themselves

in the earth, so even when the tree appears to be dead in the trunk, it continues to be fed by the branches that are rooted. Thus it grows again. Sacred to the ancestors, groves of yews sheltered ancient rituals of life and death. Yews are still being planted in graveyards. In times past, churches and graveyards were created around existing groves of yew trees. Some stories are still being told that speak of yew trees growing up out of the mouths of the dead.

Yew.
A fitting tree, an apt tree to represent the World Tree that grows in the Center.
Life and death.
Roots and branches.
Above, below.
A strong connection with the rune Eihwaz.
A rune that can easily be planted in the Center.

When we step into the Center and connect with the Tree, we know the dark, that rich, magical place that exists beneath our feet, unseen.
The place of roots.
The place of nourishment.
The place of rooted stability, balance and strength.
The place where the present disappears, containing the past, so the future can rise up out of the darkness.

As you step into the Center, you will find yourself at home, here on the earth, in the middle of the great darkness, together with the Tree. It is here you can stand in wholeness and integrity,

remembering who you are, claiming your sovereignty as the
sole ruler of your own limited sphere of influence.
This is the great circle of sight where you stand in your Center,
as all life exists in its own Center.
This is the Circle of Life.

Take up your staff.
Step into the Center.
Connect with the Tree.
Always begin in the Center.

Who am I?
Where am I?
What time is it?
What do I need?
Which way is the wind blowing?

THE STAFF

If you do not already have a staff, get one. It is a powerful tool
to use when working with rune wisdom and the Circle of Life
and a visceral way to connect your body with the Tree With
Many Names, the Tree that grows in the Center.

Once you set your intention, be alert to the various ways a staff
can come into your life.

You may decide to buy one or you can make one.

You might be given a staff by a friend.

You may find one while walking in nature, offered up to you by
a tree.

Use a walking stick or a broom handle or a ski pole until you
find something that truly speaks to you and your connection to
the runes and the Circle.

Use your imagination if that is all that is available.

Whenever you step into the Center, use your staff.

The use of a staff in claiming the Center provides us with an
ancestral connection to the staff carrying wise women in the
Norse tradition, women associated with trance and incantation.
Their knowledge of past and future connected them to the
Nornir. These women were seers, able to converse with the
unseen ones. They often sat out at night, on a hill or mound,
communing with the darkness and the dead. There are some
historical references to a Germanic rite called *sitting-listening*.
The seer sat elevated in order to know the future. Such a
vantage point offered her a broader view of the horizon, the
circle of sight.

Was the staff carrying völva listening for the sounds of
the runes?
Was her staff a way to hold onto the World Tree?
Did it provide a third leg for balance, symbolizing the three
roots of the Tree growing down into the Wells?
It could be that the staff's power was its connection to the
World Tree, the Tree With Many Names. This connection to the
framework of the Yawning Void provided a way to guard
and listen.

The importance and seniority of the völva is clearly referenced
in the *Völuspá*, the Prophecy of the Völva. Odin went two times
to the seeress. He did not raise her from the dead. She was
sitting out as the story goes, on a hill or a mound. He brought
her gifts. She warned him not to threaten her. She put him in his
place by reminding him that if he were as wise as he claimed to
be, he would not have come to her seeking wisdom.
The staff of the völva is historically connected to the distaff, a
tool used by women in the process of spinning thread from raw
fibers. This too forms a connection with the Nornir.
The distaff side is often called the left side, the female side. The
spear side, the right side, is considered male. The staff and the
spear are both tools, symbols of different kinds of power. There
are numerous medieval miniatures that depict strong women
using distaffs as weapons in combat with men. Both the distaff
and the spear connect to the Tree. Both connect you with rune
wisdom and the Circle of LIfe.

THE WIND

Which way is the wind blowing?
A strange question perhaps yet a necessary one.
The answer can mean the difference between life and death.
Wind is the movement of air.
The movement of air creates weather.
Air is not neutral.
It surrounds us.
It is outside as well as inside.
Just as the movement of air creates the weather, the movement
of air in and out of our bodies changes our moods, our stress
levels, our circulation, our overall wellbeing.
When we inhale we take air into our bodies but not just air.
We take in all that the air carries, the fragrance of cut grass and
blossoming fruit trees, the stench and sweetness of rotting
flesh and composting soil, exhaust fumes and the pheromones
of a lover, particles of dirt and the dust of our ancestors.
Once the air is inside of us, it mixes with the essence of who we
are and when we exhale it carries that information out into the
world.
The food we have eaten.
The beverages we have consumed.
The state of our emotions and the general condition of our
health.
Our inhalations and exhalations are the movement of air.
Even the slightest breath can change the weather.

You breathe when you speak.

Does your breath change the weather?
Does your breath change the climate of your life?
Do your words change the world around you?

Winds bring the smell of rain, the bouquet of flowers.
Winds carry the ash from volcanoes and the smoke from fires.
They have personalities, temperatures, velocities.
They are the gentle breezes that come in the evening as the
sun sets.
They are bitter cold blasts from the North that freeze our breath
into ice crystals.
They are hot, dry desert winds that scour and erode.

To know the winds is to spend time outside in nature, in the
weather, in daylight and in darkness.
To know the winds requires stillness of self so we can feel them
in their gentleness and in their force.
They are alive.
Winds change the landscape.
They move the water of the oceans.
They cause trees to grow sideways and they drive the clouds.
They are beings that have been in existence longer than the
gods.

Wind.
The movement of air.
Air is our first breath in and our last breath out.
Air sustains life and air brings storms that can take life.
The movement of air is necessary.
Movement brings change.

Throughout human history winds have been named. They were named because the ancestors knew each wind as an individual, a messenger, a sentient being. These names spoke of the places from which the winds were blowing, their speed, intensity, and temperature.

Mistral. Sirocco. Santa Ana. Chinook. Foehn.

Hot dry desert wind.

Icy cold north wind.

Misty ocean breeze.

These beings carry moods and emotions.

They are restless, wayward, gentle, tempestuous.

They bring weather.

Blizzards. Whirlwinds. Tornados. Fire storms. Snow storms. Hurricanes and hail.

For the ancestors in Northern Europe, knowing which way the wind was blowing was crucial to their existence, in a very literal way. Knowledge was survival. They understood that they could not control the weather or stop the wind. They needed to know how to live with it.

For these people of the far north the grandfather of all winds was Kari, the North Wind. His breath brought the ice, snow, freezing rain and bitter cold of winter. He was both feared and respected, as were his siblings, Logi, the ancient fire giant, and Aegir, lord of the seas. His offspring were Frost, Glacier and Blizzard. Snow, Frozen Snow, Snowfall, Snowdrift and Powder. There are as many kinds of wind as there are varieties of terrain.

Some like to think of them as tribes or clans coming from different directions, each group having a governing leader. For example, Kari is said to be a chieftain in Niflheim, the realm of ice.

Perhaps you have never thought about it but our lives still depend upon knowing which way the wind is blowing, both literally and figuratively.

Is there a storm brewing?
Can you smell rain?
Is the temperature about to change, perhaps drastically?
Is the wind driving a fire that is burning out of control?
Or a hurricane or a tornado?
Do you need to take cover?

An intimacy with the wind requires a high degree of awareness and attention, an intimacy with place and energies, and a certain stillness within your self.

When the wind blows in the Center of your life, what does it feel like?
From which direction does it blow?
Does it swirl around you like a cyclone or a tornado?
Is it loud, perhaps demanding attention?
Is it warm and gentle, soothing and refreshing, or is it forceful and noisy?
Does it howl or whisper?
If you were a tree, would the wind gently rock your branches or break them?
Would it scatter your leaves or tear them away?
Would it uproot you and expose what is hidden below?
Would it cause you to grow sideways as you lean away?
What is its name?
What questions would you ask it?

What ancient wisdom does it carry?
How does it affect you?
Do you get restless?
Do you feel peaceful?
Do you hear music?
What experiences do you have?
Gentle caresses or biting cold?
Do you turn your back and turn up your collar?
Do you face it and walk into the storm?

I currently live in Portland, Oregon, in the Pacific Northwest of the United States. I am familiar with the winter wind that howls down the Columbia River Gorge. I often wonder about its relationship with Kari.

WINDS OF CHANGE

The winds are alive.
Everything is alive.
Perhaps we should ask the winds what they are doing with
regard to the earth at this time.
What part are they playing in changing temperatures?
Ask the winds that bring the weather what they are up to
now?

In times past, glaciers covered much of the earth.
They melted.
They reformed.
Countless creatures appeared and disappeared.
Great changes are occurring again.
Glaciers are melting again.
This has happened before.
The earth maintains her balance with water. She is refilling
the aquifers.
Could a relationship with the North Wind help us understand
ice and the Isa rune and Laguz, the rune of flowing water?

Our Northern European creation story is a story of melting ice.
As the ice is melting now, what is being created?
As the ice is melting, what is being revealed?
Instead of being afraid of the warming should we not
instead be seeking ways to regain confidence in and rebuild
relationship with the winds? Ask them to teach us how to
survive times of great change.

The change that is occurring cannot be stopped, nor does it need to be.

It is bigger than we are and serves a purpose greater than we understand.

Stars can only be seen when it is dark.

What can only be seen when the glaciers melt?

What does it mean to be at the mercy of the winds, which is also being at the mercy of the weather?

There is a tendency for modern folk to forget their helplessness in the face of change and to imagine somehow that the elements can be controlled.

We are always helpless in the presence of the untamed, primal beings of nature.

This sense of helplessness is currently being intensified.

We are helpless in the face of a storm.

We are helpless if we cannot start a fire.

We are helpless if we cannot stop a fire.

We are helpless when the topsoil of the earth is being blown away.

And when we are at sea, we are at the mercy of the winds and we are helpless whether there are gales or doldrums.

How many of the great natural disasters are caused by or involve the wind?

Name them.

Tornados, hurricanes, cyclones, floods, forest fires.

The wind dances with earth.

The wind dances with the water.

The wind dances with fire.

Stand in the Center.
Claim your sovereignty.
Accept your helplessness.
Listen and wait.

THE RUNES ARE CALLING

The Tree was there in the beginning, in the Yawning Void,
Ginnungagap.
The roots and trunk and branches.
The Wells were there also, guarded by the Nornir.
The runes were there, all of them, unable to be counted,
numberless like the stars. These primal beings of sound are the
whispers that moved across the surface of the waters of the Wells.
They are the breathing in and out of the darkness that causes
the Web to shimmer.

These simple markings we know today as runes, these staves,
these straight lines, vertical, horizontal and diagonal, are the
flattened signatures of ancient beings.

They did not enter the story.
They are the story.

You must sit with them in silence, listening and feeling.
Over time, with great patience, stillness and willingness you
may come into relationship with these rune beings, come to
recognize their sounds, their vibrations and know when you,
your life, your body and your breath, are in alignment and
harmony with their primal wisdom.
And you will know when you are not.
These beings are the forces of creation and nature.
They are neither good nor bad.
They are neither dangerous nor safe.
Moral nor corrupt.

And surely they are not merciful or even gentle for that matter,
as is stated in one book's description of the runes.
They are indifferent.

Isa in winter enthralls you in preservation and death.
Ingwaz swells with new life in spring, awaiting harvest in autumn.
Berkana gives birth and then eats her defective young.
Teiwaz pierces loyalty with the price of compromise.
Ansuz speaks of the destructive and creative power of words.

At this time, we only know a handful of runes. There are
countless more waiting to be revealed as the ice melts.
For instance, Laguz is called the rune of water.
Water takes many forms.
Salt water and fresh.
Stagnant and flowing.
Rivers and waterfalls, ponds, lakes and wells.
Water changes form. It moves from liquid into solid or mist. It
appears as ice, snow, fog, clouds, sheets of rain and hail.
When air interacts with water, temperatures change and water
becomes weather.
Are there runes for all these different aspects of water?
Is Laguz a rune for pure water?
If so, is there a different rune for salt water that has perhaps
been forgotten or hidden away?
Is there a rune for the North Wind?
There is much for us to remember.

Viewing the runes as a mere alphabet dishonors who they are.
Worse yet, suggesting that they are an Old Italic script with

origins among the peoples of the Mediterranean perpetuates a distortion of historical evidence.

Why do we continue telling the worn-out stories about the runes that have been contrived by the conquerors, filtered through the lens of patriarchal spirituality and perpetuated in the hallowed halls of higher learning?

Why do we continue to believe that culture moved from the South to the North?

There is mounting evidence to the contrary.

What happened to our stories?

What happened to our gods?

My seven-year-old grandson is coming home from school with stories, asking me if I know that there are gods of fire and the ocean.

He proceeds to name the Greek and Roman gods we all know so well.

I tell him we are people of the North.

We have our own stories.

We have our own gods.

He listens with his eyes.

I name Surt and Aegir, Ran and Skadi.

I tell him we must remember who we are.

We must tell our own stories.

Why is classical Greek and Roman mythology still the dominant teaching?

Why do we continue to know more about the spiritual heritage of the South and the East than we do about the North?

It is time for the lost teachings of the runes to return, with intensity and brilliance.

Do not be fooled by the simplicity of the markings.
The runes were not invented.
They are signatures of sentient beings who were present at the beginning, forming and informing.
Over time they have been flattened and desiccated by historians and Odinists alike.
Put them back into the Wells.
Rehydrate them so we can see once again their multi-dimensional, crystalline structures.
Listen to their wisdom as they vibrate and shimmer in the Web.

It is my belief that those of us who are being called by the runes have a sacred obligation and responsibility to honor these traditions and bring back awareness of the rich ancestral heritage of the North.
It takes effort and questioning, exploration and digging to find this forgotten heritage and reconnect with our own indigenous ancestors.
It is a worthy endeavor.
Why is it that so many European Americans, and Europeans as well, are fascinated by and engaged in Native American spiritual and cultural practices?
Is this eagerness to adopt the beliefs and gods of others fueled by popularity and ease of accessibility?
Are we longing for something we have forgotten we even had?
Ancient spiritual practices carry wisdom. They were formed during specific times in history, in the context of a sacred languages, in geography of place that had its own gods, spirits of the land, unseen ones as well as animals and plants.

When we return to our own tribal, indigenous roots of the Motherland of Old Europe we can set aside concerns of cultural appropriation.

Are you being called by the runes and the ancestors to remember the lost teachings?

Walking this path can be challenging. The written information is sparse and what is available has come down to us second, third or even fourth hand. The translators and scribes were rarely observers much less participants and certainly not believers. They were often monks cloistered within the structure and ideology of the Christian Church or Romans writing second-hand accounts from the perspective of the conquerors.

Occasionally we can find hints of mystery and indigenous wisdom tucked between the lines, written against the grain as marginalia or preserved in riddles or kennings.

Did the gods play a part in hiding some of the wisdom in plain sight so it is easy to overlook?

You cannot rely solely on what was written.
You must call upon the ancestors and the gods to instruct and guide you.
They are waiting to be asked.
The unseen ones spoke to humans in times past.
They are speaking to us again.
Are you listening?

Are you being called to remember who you are and where you come from?

Then you must challenge yourself by asking questions, difficult and revealing.

Am I a Christian at heart dressed up in heathen garb, still using the language of a monotheist?

Do I spend more time talking about what I believe than I do living in harmony with it?

Do I go to the ancestors and the gods first?

How do I interact with the countless spirit beings who are more than human, the land wights, the spirits of water and weather?

Do I lump everything together, all the gods and goddesses, saying they are all the same, they are all one?

Does my fear of offending someone, or my need to be politically correct, inhibit the way I speak about my heritage and my ancestors?

Am I willing to challenge people's comfort zones?

Am I willing to challenge my own?

What actually do I believe?

CREATION DESTRUCTION

We are living in times that are exciting, frightening and
confusing.
The earth is changing.
It has changed before.
The ice is melting.
This is not the first time.
Creatures are becoming extinct.
This is not the first extinction nor will it be the last.

Perhaps things are occurring more rapidly.
Perhaps not.
Compared to what?
We know very little about the eons of existence of the earth.
We imagine we know more.
We are in the middle of something so we have no way of
knowing how it will unfold and what the end will be.
What we do know is that something enormous is happening.
The earth is breathing, generating and disassembling.
She is shaking, burning and flushing.

We are being manipulated by the headlines of one-sided
stories of catastrophe.
The universe is shrinking.
Stars are disappearing.
Ice is melting.
Extinction is happening.
The end is near.

Such negative presentation of the news implies that this is the only time throughout billions of years of existence that such things have happened.

Do we puny, insignificant humans actually imagine that this time in history should be or even could be the only time when nothing would drastically change, when nothing would be destroyed or become extinct?

That is ludicrous.

Broaden your perspective.

Stop running in panic and fear.

Stop repeating what you hear.

Stop awfulizing.

Ask questions.

Ask different questions.

What else is happening?
What else is possible?

When we fixate on only one thing, we create imbalance.

It is true that drastic change is occurring.

Some of it is frightening.

Some of it is sad.

Change always brings the death of what has been.

And change always brings the birth of something new.

Can we be in awe?

Can we be amazed?

Can we see the beauty that is unfolding in the presence of destruction?

Do not fall prey to thinking that one thing is good and another bad.

All things happen simultaneously.
Life just is and it affects us all in different ways.
One person's loss is another's gain.
The wolf kills the reindeer.
It kills to stay alive.
Are we the hunted or the hunter?
Do we turn to the left or to the right?
Is something being born or is it dying?
Are the gods good and the giants bad?
Does it matter if the runes are right side up or inverted?

When we stand in the Center of our own life and face the
horizon, turning in different directions, we experience all of it.
Life emerges and evolves, then dies and is transformed.
Over and over again.

When something is created or emerges it comes into form.
It then evolves. It might be easy to stumble over the word
evolve because of the way evolution is commonly taught and
presented. There is a tendency to imply and believe that when
things evolve they are always becoming better or higher. This
is a popular viewpoint but when we think of evolution as only
meaning higher or better, we lose the subtlety of the actual
word and the process.
The word itself means to develop gradually over a period of
time. Its Latin root means to unfold or to unroll.
Life rolls itself out over a gradual period of time until it
reaches the point where it is done, finished and needs to be
broken down or destroyed. And in that destruction comes the
transformation that is necessary to generate the next unfolding.

The idea that evolution only makes things better is really not true. Life unfolds differently, not necessarily better or higher. It adapts. But most people do not speak about evolution in this way. Rarely do they stop to consider what actually happens. The fact is that when anything emerges, unfolds and evolves, it will eventually destruct. This happens so it can transform and reemerge.

Thus evolution is part of the extinction process.

Ask questions.
Ask different questions.
Is extinction happening today because the changes on the earth will necessitate an unfolding of something new and different?
Is the earth evolving, going through its own cycles of generation, evolution, destruction and transformation?

When we move back and forth between destruction and creation we enter into the realm of the Jotunfolk, the primal giants who were there at the beginning and who will be there at the ending, which will be another beginning.
These giants are here right now, in the present moment, participating in the comings and goings of the universe.
They are making their presence felt and known.
They are reminding us of their existence in ways that can no longer be ignored.
It is time we start paying attention.

There are dozens of books on the shelves that speak about the runes and the gods. Very few give mention to the Jotunfolk, the primal giants.

And when the giants are written about, they are often maligned or demonized, portrayed as beings who are vile, destructive, unwanted and unwelcome. They are somehow less than the gods.

In fact, there are some heathen communities that openly express animosity toward the Jotunfolk and any who are called to honor them or even associate with them.

Does our fear of change, destruction and death find a parallel in the way we view the giants?

Does it taint our relationship with the runes?

We cannot view the giants solely as our evil, vile enemies any more than we can make the runes all peace, love and light.

Such thinking perpetuates the lie.

Runes are harsh and gentle.

Dark and light.

Life and death.

The Jotunfolk are chaotic and orderly.

They are present in all destruction and creation.

They are our ancestors.

They are also the ancestors of the gods.

When you come to the giants, when you come to the runes, when you come seeking the lost teachings, always come with questions.

This book is a question.

This book is a story.

Where did you enter the story?

What would happen if someone else told the story?

What could be uncovered if it was told from a different perspective?

Whose interests are being served when a tale is told a certain way?

Who is benefiting from these one-sided stories that manipulate and control the thinking and emotions of the masses?

What is beyond the horizon?

What is beneath our feet?

What is hidden, waiting to be revealed?

2

DIRECTIONS
OF THE WHEEL

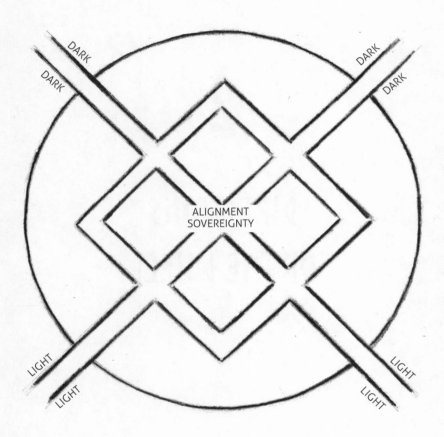

CENTER

Alignment

Sovereignty

Courage

Integrity

Honor

Power

LOST

We are a people who have lost our way.
In order to know where we are going, we must know where we
come from.
In order to know where we come from, we must know who we are.
In the past, when the ancient ones lost their way, they would
come to the fire and listen.
The fire was the center of the circle.
The circle was the horizon.
The circle was a wheel.
We begin in the Center.
We always begin in the Center.
We must return to the Center.
This is the wisdom of the runes and the lost teachings of the
Wheel.

Those of us with Northern European ancestry have indigenous
tribal roots. Our ancestors of the North dressed in furs and
animal skins. Their bodies were marked with ink and scars.
Feathers dangled from their tangled, braided hair. They beat their
drums with antlers, bones and sticks, performed rituals, danced
around sacred fires and communed with spirit beings and the
dead. They altered their consciousness with fermented drinks,
plant medicines and mushrooms. They lived in harmony with
the earth, honored her cycles, rhythms and seasons. They killed
animals in order to survive and prospered in climates of extreme
cold and months of darkness. They were strong, resourceful
people who lived with honor and courage. Their blood flows in
our veins and we carry their memory in our bones.

It is time for us to remember who we are and find our way back to our own indigenous, tribal heritage. Instead of being fascinated with and fixated on the traditions and religions of others, it is time for us to reconnect with our own spiritual wisdom, the forgotten wisdom of the North, the lost teachings of the runes.

How sad and disturbing it is that most people today only know the runes through sensationalized stories of Viking violence, fantasy fiction and video games. They associate them with the Nazi party and heavy metal bands. The New Age and Neo-pagan communities use them for fortune telling and divination and there is even a site on the Internet that makes the statement,

they're just letters, folks. Nothing to get excited about.

The common and popular belief, even among some of the Heathen kin, is that the runes are limited in number, usually 24, organized into groups and lined up in a specific sequence, as if they are merely an alphabet. They are spoken of solely in relationship to Odin, the so-called All Father High God and the study of them relies most heavily on the writings of the 13th century scholar, politician, Snorri Sturluson. He collected and translated from sources that had been written long after Christianization.
It is no surprise that his work would carry the taint of a monotheistic, non-believer.

Are we believers or do we have a monotheistic gaze?
Have we lost sight of the possibility that the rune beings, our

ancestors and the unseen ones speak to us today and impart
information and wisdom that was never written down?
This is not such a strange or foreign concept.
The gods, the unseen ones and the dead have always spoken
to us.

Living in harmony with the ancient wisdom of the runes
requires courage and a willingness to live from the Center, a
place of honor, accountability and truth.
From the Center we can face in any direction and find answers
from the past that can guide us into the future.

When you have lost your way you must stop, take a breath and
step into the Center, your Center, the Center of your life.

Take up your staff.
Find the horizon.
Orient yourself.
Stand with integrity.
Claim your sovereignty.

Doing this will in no way lessen or diminish anyone or anything
for each of us is the Center of the circle of our own life.

The Tree With Many Names

In the Center of the circle stands the World Tree, a mystery tree.
Some call it Yggdrasil, a name that ties the Tree to Odin and
his sacrifice to gain access to rune wisdom. Others know it as
Laerath, the Listener or possibly the Guardian.
Is it an ash tree?

Is it a yew?

Is it possible that this mighty World Tree exists as all trees, showing itself in different ways at different times, allowing us to be with it, in the moment?

There is much to learn about this mystery Tree.

Its roots wind their way down through all the Nine Worlds.

The Nornir, with faces hidden, dwell in these roots, guarding the Wells, tending the Tree, carving the runes into its bark and smearing it with healing clay.

To be sure, this Tree was there at the beginning, which was also the ending.

It was being cared for by the Nornir long before Odin appeared on the scene.

Of course its original name would not be linked to Odin.

As the Listener, what does it hear?

As the Guardian, what does it guard?

Does it listen through its roots, feeling the vibrations of all Nine Worlds?

Does it guard what is coming into form?

Does it know the ending before it arrives?

Standing in the Center of the circle, connecting with the World Tree, is a powerful way to find balance. The Tree shows us how to be grounded, rooted and centered while at the same time, expansive, open and growing.

To stand in the Center with the World Tree is to experience, through your body, the wisdom of the ages.

What is above is the same as below.

We have forgotten our connection with the earth and nature.
We have been severed from our tribal, indigenous roots.
We suffer from inherited ancestral grief.
We feel lost and confused, ungrounded and out of balance
because we have been cut off from our own spirituality.
We must return to the Center, our Center, the place of our
individual sovereignty.

There are many of us who were raised in monotheistic, religious
environments where we were taught to denounce our beautiful,
sensuous, sexual bodies. We were told our bodies were sinful
and imperfect, inferior somehow to god. We were told we
needed to be saved. We were told we needed a savior. We were
told we could never be perfect unless we believed.
Are we still enthralled by monotheism and belief in the need of
a savior?

There are some who espouse transcendence, constantly
striving for higher consciousness as if our beautiful, animal
bodies and the earth are somehow inferior.
As if we need to get away.
Why are we always striving to get away?
Why would we want to believe that this glorious, abundant,
awe-inspiring earth is merely a testing ground and we only
come here to learn lessons by experiencing struggle, difficulty
and pain?
Such thinking cuts us off not only from our bodies but from the
earth and nature as well.
Is it any wonder we are always out of balance?

The lost teachings of the runes show us how to reconnect our minds with the wisdom of our bodies and our inner knowing, remembering that higher is not better than lower, that spiritual is not better than physical. We learn to celebrate our humanness, our carnal nature and return to balance. This is the gift of the Center. This is the gift of the Tree. Its roots grow deep into the body of the earth. Its branches reach up into the sky. It is always connected by the trunk.

The Squirrel, The Dragon And The Eagle

According to legend, there are many creatures that live in the World Tree. One of them is Ratatoskr, the squirrel. This clever little being runs up and down the trunk, carrying messages back and forth from the eagle and the falcon that dwell in the topmost branches to the dragon serpent Nidhogg that crawls among its roots, always gnawing on them.

The imagery of these beings provides us with a wealth of knowledge. As we stand in the Center of our own life, connected with the Tree, we find balance by being rooted in the earth and open to the sky. The scurrying of the squirrel reminds us of the need for integrated communication between our minds and our bodies, and reinforces our need for far-seeing perspective as well as dark, hidden nourishment.

Many of the stories present the dragon serpent as being bad or evil, implying that she is trying to destroy the Tree by chewing on its roots. Nidhogg also engages in another seemingly undesirable activity. She frequently crawls over the roots onto Dead Man's Shore where she eats corpses. This of course feeds into the belief that the things above are good and the things below are bad.

When we step into the Center and connect with the Tree and these creatures, we are reminded that nothing in life can function outside the natural cycle of things. Removal of dead wood encourages and stimulates new growth. As for the eating of corpses, the truth is that the rot and consumption that occur around death are a necessary part of new life.
Life comes from death.
Life feeds upon death.
This is the mystery.

Step into the Center with your staff.
Embrace the Tree.
Feel the squirrel connecting your mind and body.

What are you able to see on the horizon from the vantage place of the eagle and the falcon?
They are birds of prey.
They are birds of death.
Are you perhaps surveying the countryside looking for something to kill so you can live?
How could this perspective serve you at this time?

What is happening for you down below the surface?
Are you being fed, nourished and watered through your roots, through your connectedness with the dark places of the earth beneath your feet?
What things need to be buried so they can rot, decompose and be reused?

Such questions could lead you to the Ear rune and the wisdom of sacrifice and burial.

Standing in the Center with the Tree might support you in realizing unique aspects of your own nature or perhaps bring into your awareness places in your life where there is a disconnect or imbalance or maybe even lingering beliefs and attitudes about above being better than below, or up being more spiritual than down or even life being more important than death.

Are you a communicator?
Do you have a knack for connecting things, perhaps things that might appear to be at odds with each other?
Is your nature busy and energetic?
Are you far seeing?
Do you have a broad perspective?
What do you believe about death and decay?
Do you find beauty and necessity in things that take place below the surface, in the dark?

Using The Staff

There is no right kind of staff. It can be long or short, thick or thin, heavy or light. You may feel drawn to a wooden staff because it holds the energy of the Tree. Trust yourself. You will know what is right for you.

As written about earlier, wise women in the Northern Traditions were staff carriers. They were healers and seers who often wandered the land.

Learning to use a staff, walk with a staff, work with a staff will connect you to these foremothers. It will give you strength and balance.

Do you feel unsteady or ungrounded?
Have you lost your way?
Are you facing a major decision or choice?
Do you feel confused, overridden, unsure, frustrated?
Are you longing for a sense of confidence and direction?
Take hold of your staff and step into the Center.
It does not matter where you are or who you are.
It does not matter whether you can do it physically or only with your imagination.
Just do it and declare,

I am stepping into the Center of my own life, with my staff and I reclaim my sovereignty, my courage, my integrity and my power.

This might feel awkward or uncomfortable at first. Over time, as you practice it, you will gain a determined sense of yourself and experience the great rush of power that comes from claiming ownership of and responsibility for your life, supported by the power of the staff.

Your feet and your staff create a beautiful triad, a meaningful way to align with the three main roots of the World Tree and the three Wells hidden in the roots and the Nornir, the triple being who dwells in the roots guarding the Wells.

I Am The Center

Stand with your staff and declare,

I am the center of the universe.

I realize such a statement goes against the grain for many of us but the truth is that at any given moment, no matter who you are or where you are, you are the Center. Everything, space and time, goes out from you in all directions and because there is no end point, you are always in the Center. When you stand up and claim this for yourself you cannot and do not take anything away from anyone. You are not standing in their body or in their life. Each and every one of us is our own Center. Making such a claim means recognizing who you are and how you must be in order to live with honor, courage, integrity and truth.

When you stand on the top of a hill and turn your body around, looking in all directions, what you see is a circle. Everything extends out and away from you. How you position yourself in the circle is in relationship to time, but time not as a mental concept but time as the experience of what you are actually seeing. The circle you see is the horizon and you orient yourself within the circle by noticing where the sun and the moon rise and where they set. You know what time it is in the present moment by your body's orientation with the horizon.

If you stayed long enough on the top of this hill you would begin to notice that the place where the sun rises and where it sets and how it arcs across the sky changes slightly each day. Over time, you would notice a pattern. If you watched the sky at night, you would see that the stars above you also move in a pattern.

When you orient yourself in the present moment, in the Center of your own life, you begin to understand that you cannot separate your location from the experience of time because you can only know where you are in relationship to what is happening around you on the earth.

Learn to use your physical body and all of your senses.
Ask yourself these questions,

What am I feeling right now?
What am I seeing, hearing, smelling?
What am I experiencing?
Which way is the wind blowing?
What is the temperature?
Is it dark or is it light?

You experience life through your body.
You cannot experience it any other way.
Even when you think you are doing it with your mind, all sensations still come to you through your body and all of your senses act in unison at the same time.
You cannot separate them.
Living from the Center is living from your whole self not just from the place of your thoughts.

Our ancestors were people of the land, intimately familiar with the earth. They spoke about life as they experienced it through their senses. They saw the sun rise up out of the earth.

They saw it disappear. They watched the sky circle above them.
The sun still rises and the sun still sets.
Is that not what you see?
We still use the same language to describe what we see in spite
of the explanations we have been give by the so-called experts.
Exploring the lost teachings of the runes gives us an
opportunity to consider the words we use to explain life
and the words we use to describe what we are actually
experiencing.

Orient

Most of us use words and repeat phrases without giving much
thought to their origins and original meanings. For example,
the word *orient*. It is a word with a Latin root and it carries the
meaning of rising or rising up. For the Latin-speaking people
of ancient Rome, *orient*, as a noun, was the East, the place of
the rising sun. When they faced the rising sun, they faced the
direction of Asia. For them, Asia was the Orient and they called
the people who inhabited those lands Orientals.

When used as a verb, one of its meanings is to find your place
in relation to your surroundings. It is quite fascinating when you
think about it. We still *orient* ourselves by facing the rising sun
but what is East of us is relative to and dependent upon where
we live. I currently live in Portland, Oregon on the West coast of
the United States. If I face the direction of the rising sun, I could
truthfully refer to New York as the Orient and the people living
there as Orientals. Actually, I would have to turn and face the
West in order to be looking in the direction of the part of the world
now commonly referred to as Asia, formerly known as the Orient.

We still use the word as a way to describe how we position ourselves on earth. It is interesting to note that at one time in history maps were drawn in such a way that East, the place of the rising sun, was shown at the top, instead of North. It is not unlikely that throughout human history people would have referenced their place of being in relationship to the sun. There is a beautiful expression found in Old German. It speaks of the East as the Morning Land.

Eihwaz And Yew

As mentioned earlier, the Eihwaz rune aligns easily with the Center. There is no top or bottom to this rune. It is a mirror image of itself. It is a rune of balance, of death and life, down and up, bottom and top, always turning, always spinning. Eihwaz whispers to us that we must find the wisdom that is held in the dark as well as the wisdom that is evident in the light.
You can bring Eihwaz with you into the Center when you want to reconnect your mind with your body so you feel as much and as often as you think.

Eihwaz is often connected to the yew tree, a tree sacred to our ancestors. Groves of yews were mysterious gathering places where rituals involving sexual intercourse, birthing and dying occurred, often simultaneously. The branches of the yew trees grow up and then back down into the earth, creating unique enclosures where consciousness can be altered by the mildly hallucinogenic vapors exhaled by this tree of life and death. Most parts of the yew are poisonous, and yet it is a tree that appears to live, almost forever.

In Europe and the British Isles, it is common to see yew trees growing in graveyards and cemeteries that are adjacent to Christian churches. In some cases, the yews have been planted there. But more likely than not, the church was built directly on top of or adjacent to an ancient, sacred grove.

As you become more familiar and comfortable with the teachings of the Wheel you will come to appreciate that you can bring any one of the runes into the Center and see how its wisdom can be used to restore balance, to ground and root, to rise and expand.

Opposites

Are you familiar with the kind of pseudo-spiritual thinking that assigns moralistic values to words?

Have you been maneuvered, perhaps subtly, to view light as better than dark or high as better than low?

What about up and down or right and left?

Have you been told to raise your vibrations, reach for higher consciousness and strive for the light because such things are better, perhaps even more spiritual?

Are you familiar with this kind of jargon and use of words?

Such thinking is harmful. When we focus only on the light and high vibrations and transcendence, we create imbalance and when we are out of balance our life does not work. Standing in the Center and aligning with Eihwaz requires that we bring ourselves back down to earth and embrace the slow, rhythmic heartbeat of the mother.

I invite you to lower your vibrations, seek endarkenment and dig deep into the dense, fertile richness of the earth.
This too is spiritual.

What is your response to such an invitation and why?

If you carry even the slightest hint of a belief that low vibrations and darkness are bad, inferior or evil and that you constantly need to avoid them, you might feel quite uncomfortable with such an invitation, perhaps even a bit afraid.

I frequently hear people talk about returning to the place they believe they came from, a place of infinite light where they are pure energy, confident that such a place is better somehow than the earth.

Why would someone believe that their physical, sensuous body is inferior and that being pure energy and light would be better than having form?
Where does that belief originate?
Who says that energy is light?
Is it perhaps dark?

Why would anyone want to leave the pleasures and enjoyment of a sensuous life?
The luxuriousness of touch, taste, and smell.
The ability to caress a lover's body or inhale the freshness of new life as you cradle an infant in your arms.
The lusciousness of a ripe peach, fine wine, heather in the highlands, the fragrance of jasmine and honeysuckle, or snowflakes or birdsong or moonlight on the still waters of a lake.

Where is it that they want to go?
Where do they want to be that they imagine would be better?

Rune wisdom brings us back into harmony with all of life, our
bodies and the earth included.
When we stand in the Center, completely present in our bodies,
we can truly appreciate that the sun appears and disappears
and that the dark leaves and returns.
We embrace the truth of the constant movement that is present
in balance.
We no longer consider dark as bad nor light as good.
We come to understand that we do not need to shine light into
the dark.
It lacks nothing.
It exists as its own being, full and rich, allowing us to see and
experience things we cannot see and experience in the light.
The void, Ginnungagap, is dark.
The tiny specks of light come and go.
The darkness remains.
The dark and the light exist as separate beings, each whole and
complete.
Light does not need to be enriched with darkness nor does the
dark need to be enlightened.

In the stories told by our Northern ancestors, night was a
giantess whose name was Nott and it was she who gave birth
to Jord, the earth. Earth is the mother, from whose body we
emerge and the body to which we return. So in the telling of
this story, night is our grandmother.
This is the beautiful balance that is found in the lost teachings
of the runes.

As Above So Below

What are your thoughts about the above statement?
What do you believe?
How does that belief manifest in your daily life?

There are practices within some traditions that place greater importance and value on what is believed to be spiritual. Such practices often carry with them the idea that the physical body is somehow inferior, corrupt, and we need to get away from it, transcend it. There are certain ascetic doctrines that denounce pleasures such as sex, the enjoyment of eating, drinking and celebrating and even the showing of emotions. Self-denial, self-mortification, austerity are believed to be the way to attain high spiritual states and ultimately enlightenment.
Deprivation is considered a virtue.

What deadening damage is caused by religions that denounce sex and sexuality, preaching instead that such tendencies are sinful and should be controlled with rigid rules of abstinence and punitive laws? What harm is inflicted upon us by religions that deny the spirituality of the body, saying that normal, natural functions such as menstruation, birth, arousal, climax, pleasure, passion and death are bad or somehow less than spiritual? How do such teachings affect the way you feel about your body?

All expressions of life are equal.
Life is physical.
Life is spiritual.
The two cannot be separated.

One is not more important than the other.
One is not better than the other.
The spiritual is not above.
The physical is not below.
We are not a spirit having a body experience nor are we a body having a spirit experience.
We are alive.
It is not possible for us to be separate from nature any more than it is possible for us to divide ourselves into parts.

There is always balance and fluid movement. We see this and know it in nature. There is time for great stillness, calm, serenity and peace. There are eruptions, earthquakes and violence. There are fallow fields and trees heavy with fruit. Things sprout, grow, blossom, flower and go to seed. Things ripen, rot, putrefy, dissolve and decay. There is abundance and there is lack. There is killing and there is sustaining. Life is all of this, over and over again. Life is physical and life is spiritual. Our indigenous ancestors knew this and lived in harmony with the wisdom.

We cannot live by being just the leaves and branches that reach up into the sky enjoying the sun and swaying in the wind. We must also be the roots that find their way down deep into the earth, twisting and growing around rocks and boulders, seeking nutrients and water, knowing intimately the small things, the bugs and worms and decay.

As above, so below. There is no difference.
Stepping into the Center challenges us to examine any underlying, unspoken, perhaps unacknowledged beliefs that the dark and hidden things below are bad, evil and most

decidedly dangerous.

We are taught to fear and push such things away. Even in our language words such as lower, base, below and down carry negative connotations.

Such beliefs and fears keep us off center, out of balance in the same way believing in the separation of the physical and spiritual does.

Is it any wonder we often feel lost?

The Wisdom Of The Center

When you find yourself living too much in your head, overthinking things, trying too hard to figure things out with your mind, take your staff, step into the Center and ask yourself these questions,

What do I think I should do?
What do I feel I need to do?
What does my head say?
What does my body say?
What do I feel in my gut?
What do I know in my heart?

As you ask yourself these questions notice where the answers come from. Notice also if you place any judgment or negativity on some answers, or perhaps trust or value some more than others because of where they come from.

If you are contemplating something and thinking about it only in a linear manner you might wish to bring the Dagaz rune into the Center and see what insights you can gain from it about the cycles of life, the continuum of a circle and the endless turning of the Wheel. Dagaz is a rune that can be inverted or reversed and stay the same. It holds the teaching of transformation, of movement from one thing into another. Each side of Dagaz is separate and yet, at the same time, both sides make up the whole.

The shape of Dagaz can represent night and day. The vertical line on one side being high noon and the vertical line on the opposite side midnight. The movement from night into day and back again is the movement of two things that are separate and equal and part of a whole. The still point in the middle is the moment of transformation.

What happens when you live life in this way?

Are there times when you feel off-balance and out of sorts?
Are you lacking joy and pleasure?
Do you need to slow down, take more time to savor life and enjoy food?
Do you need to celebrate your body and all of your senses?
Are you spending too much time indoors and in your head, not spending enough time, or any time, out in nature?
Do you dwell in the past or obsess about the future?
Have you forgotten you are sovereign in your own life and responsible for the choices and decisions you make?

Step into the Center.
Find the horizon as it circles around you.
Bring in the runes, one by one.
Ask them individually and collectively how to align with the World Tree.

Ask them to share their wisdom regarding life and death, light and dark, above and below.

You arrange your thoughts in relationship to where you are and what time it is.
You cannot separate place, which is the present moment, from what you are experiencing.
Whenever you find yourself caught in a crazy, spinning frenzy of too much thinking,
take your staff, step back into the Center, and reclaim your power.
Ask yourself the questions,

Who am I?
Where am I?
What time is it?
Which way is the wind blowing?
What do I need?

The Center is the place of power.
The Center is the place of courage.
The Center is the place of integrity and honor.
We must have these in order to live in balance and harmony.
Stand in the Center and declare,

I am the sovereign, the sole ruler of my limited sphere of influence and as the sovereign I am responsible for my own life and the decisions I make. I am not powerless.

Once you begin to embody this practice, you will live with a very different perspective and experience.

Remembering The Future Foretelling The Past

Stand in the Center in the present moment with your staff and claim your sovereignty.

What do you observe?
What do you realize and experience?

Notice the clouds in the sky and along the horizon.
Feel the earth beneath your feet.
Hear the birds, smell the air, taste the wind.
All this is happening as you stay in one place and yet standing there you also know that beyond the horizon all manner of unseen things exist.
They are coming into form.
This is the future.

As you stand in the Center you can take a step in any direction, and when you do you will be able to see things that you could not see before you took the step.
You have stepped into the future.
It was already there.
It already existed.
You could not see it because it was beyond the horizon, beyond your limited circle of sight.
It was waiting to reveal itself to you.
The future already exists beyond the horizon.

The mystery is that the future also exists in the present moment. It is there in the acorn that holds the memory of how to grow into an oak tree. It is held in the egg that contains the unformed bird. Life remembers the future as it unfolds from the inside.

The mystery is that the present moment also holds the past. Consider the oak tree from which the acorn fell. The tree is there in the present moment and the past exists in the tree because it sprouted from an acorn. The past exists hidden inside the tree as well. The story of the past is told in the growth rings. Drought, fire, abundance or lack of water. Disease. All these past events are evident in the being of the tree that is alive in the present moment.

The tree holds the future as well. It grows leaves. When the leaves let go and fall they become the past because they are no longer part of the tree. Once they fall, they return to the ground where they decay and become compost. When this happens they become the future. They provide the nutrients needed by the tree to grow more leaves.

The same mysteries are held in your body. Your body standing in the Center, in the present moment, holds the future.
A woman holds the future in her body because she has the ability to give birth to new life. A man holds the future in his body because he has the ability to fertilize. And even more than that, both of them will become the future when they die. Their bodies return to the earth and decompose.
These recycled energies and elements will become new soil that will feed new growth.

All life holds the past and the future in the present moment. This is the beauty and the mystery of the cycle that exists beneath our feet, and the cycle that exists beyond the horizon that moves with us as we move with it. When you think only in a straight line about ultimate goals such as going to heaven, attaining Nirvana or reaching enlightenment, you are unable to grasp the teachings of the runes. The amazing wisdom of the cycle of return, over and over again.
Of no beginning and no ending.
No place to go away to, and no place to be from.
We are already here.

Find the balance that exists in wisdom and ask,

Where am I in this present moment as I stand in the Center of all that is?

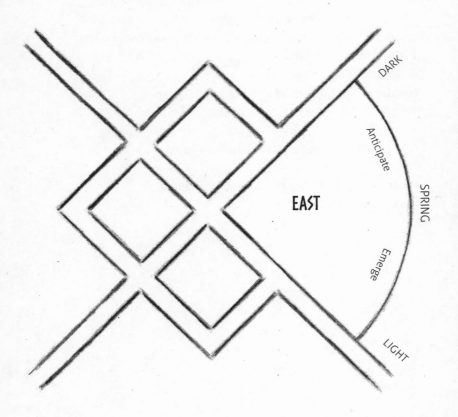

EAST

Anticipate

Emerge

Gestate

Generate

Appear

Arise

THE EAST

The place of the sunrise.
The place of birth and beginnings, of emerging, sprouting, and hatching.
East is springtime and creativity and possibility.
The release of stored energy and potential.
The moment of orgasm.
It is the place of equal dark and equal light.

How do you speak about the East?

Take your staff.
Step into the Center.
Connect with the Tree.
Remember, there is as much below as there is above.

Feel the expanse above and the movement of the wind.
Feel the ground beneath your feet.
Feel all the places where you are connected to the earth.
Feel the place from which you are nourished, the place from which you are watered.
Turn and face the direction of the dawn, the morning land, the orient, the place of rising up.
This is the place where the sun appears.
This is the place where the dark appears, as the sun is setting.
Such things are always about perspective.
There are no rules.
There is no formula.

When you stand in the Center you do not need to worry about turning in a certain way, clockwise, counterclockwise, to your right or to your left.

When you know who you are, where you are and what time it is, you can decide what you need to do to be able to face the direction of rising up, the place of emerging.

Who am I?
Where am I?
What time is it?
What do I need?
Which way is the wind blowing?

Stand still.
Listen.
Be amazed.
To face the East is to step into the place of awe and appreciation for all that begins, again and again.
Emerging is part of an endless cycle.
Emerge, unfold, harvest, transform.

Everything that comes forth in Spring exists because of the transformation that occurred in the dark of Winter.
Transformation is possible in Winter because harvest happened in Autumn.
Harvest is possible in Autumn because unfolding occurred in Summer.
Unfolding occurs because something emerged in Spring.

The Sun

The sun can appear from behind a mountain. It can rise up out of the ocean or a lake, It can rise up out of the prairie or the plains or the steppes. What you see and experience depends on where you live. What we all see in common is the sun emerging. It rises up out of the place where it has been. Rather than trying to explain what you are experiencing by repeating scientific technicalities, why not watch in awe as this enormous glowing circle of fire rises up from wherever it has been since you last saw it.

This is what you must do to know in your body the wisdom of the East.
Rise before dawn, while the sky is still dark.
Go some place with the sole intention of watching the sun emerge.

What happens?
What does it feel like?
Does the air change?
Can you feel a slight breeze?
Can you sense its warmth even if the temperature does not change?
How do you experience the departure of the dark that is happening behind you in the West, as you face the returning light in the East?

When you witness this marvel, say thank you.
Thank you for returning.
It is a bit arrogant on our part, is it not, to assume that the sun will always come back.

We do not really know, do we, when she disappears into the water or the land, where she goes because we have never gone there with her.

The ancestors know. They have gone where the sun goes, into the dark, beyond the horizon and beneath our feet. It serves us well to remember our ancestors and connect with them. They are keepers of wisdom we need in order to survive.

We do not need to imagine what they saw and experienced. We still see and experience the same things. The sun disappears as the dark returns. She goes into the earth or into the water. She is gone for varying lengths of time. In the far North, in winter, she disappears completely or stays close to the horizon. In summer she rides high in the sky. In fact, when you live close to the Arctic Circle, there is only one sunrise and one sunset during the entire year.

Birth and death are the same experiences as the coming and going of the dark and the light.
Emerging and disappearing.
A cycle.
We emerge from the place of dark, birthed from the mystery of the female body.
We disappear into the dark, into the mystery of the body of the earth.

The miracle of the rising of the sun is a repetition.
It is not a one-time thing.
It is over and over again.
It is a ritual we can participate in.

What do you do each morning to celebrate?
Start a fire, light a candle, pick a rune?

Whatever you do, whether it is the special way you make your
tea or coffee or select your favorite mug, or step outside with
your bare feet, remember your place in nature and greet the
sun when she returns.
It is said that the gods do not talk to us anymore because we no
longer believe in them.
Is this true as well about the sun?
Does the sun talk to you?

Our ancestors participated in sacred rituals that honored and
followed the movement of the sun and the seasons of the
year, not according to an arbitrary calendar but rather as life
unfolded in perfect rhythm with the earth and the heavens.
This practice brought them back to the Center, over and over
again, remembering the need to be in perfect harmony and
connection with what is above and what is below, what is
hidden and what is revealed, what is dying and what is coming
alive.

Sowelo is a rune connected to the sun. In the Northern
mysteries the sun is female. Her name is Sunna. Our ancestors
in the North paid attention to the movements of the sun. Their
lives depended upon such knowledge. They honored her
with rituals and festivals and marked her return each Winter
Solstice with special celebrations. These spiritual practices are
so deeply etched in our bones and our ancestral memories it is
impossible to remove them.

Have you ever thought about the fact that most of the imagery and customs of Christmas have nothing to do with the birth of a Middle Eastern Jew in the town of Bethlehem near the shores of the Mediterranean Sea?

Reindeer, snow, amanita mushrooms, evergreen trees, candles, elves and shamans dressed in red and white all come to us straight from the North and are part of timeless, Winter Solstice traditions that celebrate the birth of the sun.

Sowelo has a special intimacy with the sun. It carries a reminder and a warning. We depend upon the sun for light and warmth, for growth and melting and the ability to see with our eyes. However, we cannot look directly at the sun or she will blind us. The thing that allows us to see can also cause us to lose our sight.

When we stand in the Center facing the East we are reminded that light is in perfect balance with dark. They are equal and they are vital. That is why East, the place of rising up, belongs to both the light and the dark.
Take a few minutes to reflect on the necessity of both.
This wisdom is part of the lost teachings of the runes.

When was the last time you stood facing East and watched the sun rise up from beyond the horizon?
Have you ever thanked the sun for rising?
Have you ever thanked her for her return?
Have you ever thanked the dark for returning as well?

Berkana

Not only is the East the place of emerging and rising, it is also the place of birth and beginning.

Life emerges. A little sprout comes out of an acorn, a seed, or a kernel of rye, poking up through the soil. The egg emerges from the body of a chicken and a chick pecks its way out of the shell. Humans emerge from the body of their mother. It is a repetition of life in our natural, physical world.

Over and over again.

Life emerges.

New life, new growth often needs careful nurturing, protection, gentleness and attention and even with all of that in place, some new life never grows strong enough to be viable on its own. Some things need to be culled, pruned or removed. Some things need to be allowed to die. This is the wisdom of Berkana.

When new life comes forth it holds a pattern. This pattern is not fully evident at first but unfolds over time. We may doubt what is trying to be born or sprout or come forth. Its appearance in the beginning rarely resembles the form it takes in maturity. Just think about the tiny acorns from which mighty oak trees grow. The energies and teachings of the East contain an element of anticipation, hopefulness and trust and at the same time an element of uncertainty as we patiently wait for what is still unknown.

Berkana is a rune connected with the birch tree. The birch is called the Shining One, her leaves sparkling in the sun when a gentle breeze blows. Birches were some of the first trees to appear as the ice was melting at the end of the last ice age in Northern Europe.

Berkana is said to be the rune of the mother, she who gives life and she who takes it away. This is the wisdom of the direction of the East. Not all things that are birthed or brought forth can be or should be cared for, nurtured or tended. Some things need to die. In nature, the mother will push away her young if they are defective, weak or sickly. She will kill them and often eat them. This is perhaps difficult for us to imagine yet it is the wisdom of life. It is the wisdom that allows for life to remain strong and viable.

You can stand in the Center and turn to the East when you wish to evaluate something that is showing up or manifesting itself in your life.
Some things may be desirable or wanted.
Some may not.
Some may be expected.
Others may be a surprise.
Some things may not be in harmony with who you are.

Turn to the East and ask,

What is this?
Does it belong in my garden, in my life?
Is it in alignment with who I am, or does it put me off-balance?
Do I need to care for it, feed it or nurture it?
Does it need to be culled, pruned, weeded or ignored?
Should I pull it up or walk away?
Should I water it or not?

Such questions are good reminders that not everything that is birthed will survive nor should survive.
Not everything that sprouts or hatches is viable.
And sometimes, even when we want something and have waited and planned for it, it does not live.
We can tend and water.
We can protect and nourish and even with all of this there is no guarantee.
Some things emerge weak or defective.
And it could that a seed blew in and sprouted in an environment in which it cannot thrive or survive.

So when you sense that something like this is happening, turn to the East and acknowledge the truth. None of this is bad. It just is. It may be difficult or disappointing. It may be devastating or a relief. Bring these things into the East and listen for the wisdom.

Should I continue to put energy and attention into it or should I kill it or allow it to die on its own?

Call upon Berkana. She may tell you that everything is going to be okay.
Or she may tell you to let it go because it looks like it is not going to make it.
This is not easy. This could apply to something that is deeply traumatic such as a miscarriage, an abortion, an accident or a relationship. This is life that contains the truthfulness of ending.

Embrace Berkana and her wisdom. Take a lesson from her.
Beware the devouring mother. She who gives birth, nourishes,
and protects will also eat her young.

Creativity

East is a place of vision, not just literal sight but the ability to
see things with the mind's eye and the eyes of the heart.
We imagine things that do not yet have form or substance.
East is the place of creativity as well. ·
When we create we bring to life things that have not yet
occurred.
We write, paint, compose, dance.
When we create we remember the future.

When we create are we giving form to something that already
exists in the dark?
Does it live someplace beyond the horizon?
Do we call it forth or does it come in on its own, looking for
someone through whom it can manifest or materialize?
Is it waiting for the right conditions to sprout and rise up?
Is it waiting for the right person to be an instrument through
which it can be heard or seen?
If it comes to you and says "will you help me" and you ignore
it or delay, does it then go to someone else asking the same
question?
When we create or bring something into form, do we take it for
granted or think it is ours or do we stand in awe, in the East,
and thank it for birthing through us?
What do you believe?

East is not just about the rising up of the sun.
It is about creation.
What emerges in the East comes from transformation in the
North.
It is a cycle.
Where did you enter the story?

Creation Stories

Imagine being caught in a blinding blizzard. All is white. There
are no directions. There is no up or down. Suddenly, from
out of nowhere, which is everywhere, a reindeer appears, a
reindeer cow. Audhumbla. She is pregnant with twins. She gives
birth. She licks them from their birth sacs which had frozen
immediately in the cold.
She nurses them, feeding them from her own body.
They grow.
They mate with her.
She gives birth again, this time to females who will become
mothers themselves.
Audhumbla emerged.
The twins Ymir and Buri emerged.
The earth was formed from the body of Ymir who had emerged
from the body of the reindeer cow.

Our Northern ancestors could relate to such a story, a story of
emerging. They lived with such conditions. North is home to
mist and fog, ice rime and hoar frost.
North is home to the chaos of fire meeting ice, the steamy
explosions of ash that occur when volcanoes erupt under
glaciers.

Audhumbla, the primal mother reindeer cow emerged.
Ymir emerged.
Buri emerged.
Bestla emerged.

The gods make nothing.
The gods give birth to nothing.
They cannot.
Yet they try to take credit for everything that is birthed and
created from the darkness of the womb, the Yawning Void,
forgetting that they themselves emerged from the body of the
mother. They came forth from the dark.

In Norse mythology it is the dwarves who fashion magical items
of great beauty and skill, using elements they mine from the
earth.
Nothing has changed. All wealth comes from the land. This
wisdom is held in the Fehu rune.
The earth is the mother who came from the Mother.
All patriarchal systems are out of balance. With the wisdom of
Fehu. With the wisdom of the East. With the teachings of the
runes.They delude the masses with the belief that the father
creates and that life comes forth from the male.
Sadly, there are even those within the Heathen community
who insist on referring to Odin as All Father, forgetting that he
too must trace his lineage back to the Mother, Audhumbla, the
reindeer cow.
The creation stories we have been told have blatantly left out
the mother.

When we retell our own creation story, we honor the mother
and we honor the wisdom of the East.
It is the mother who gives birth.
It is from her body that life rises up.
We all come from the mother, Odin included.
In the retelling of the creation story we remember her name.

Longing

Facing East can connect us to the place of longing that exists in
us all, that place where we sense something is missing. It can
help us identify feelings of nostalgia, the desire to go home, to
return or to pursue things that have been hidden or forgotten.
Answers can rise up out of the horizon just as the sun does
after she has hidden herself through the dark of winter or the
dark of night.
You can face the East to remember.

Sometimes longing comes from the place of creative desires
or even, as Henry David Thoreau suggests, from the stirrings of
remorse that trouble us because we are living but a fraction of
our life.

Is there a place in your life where you carry stirrings of remorse
because you are not living up to your potential?
Is there a place inside you that has lost touch with your dreams
and the realm of possibility?

Sometimes longing is connected to grief and we can grieve for
something we do not even realize we have lost.

We have been cut off from our indigenous heritage, our ancestral folk connections to the earth.
We have lost our songs and our stories.
We grieve because we no longer remember who we are and because we no longer remember who our ancestors are.

Turning to the East can help us remember our songs.
Singing these forgotten songs will affect the vibration of the Web of life.
We cannot undo the past.
We must sing the songs again. The runes can help us.
They are vibrational beings. When we learn their names, we begin to say them, to sing them and to tone them. Hearing these ancient songs will activate our memories and help us understand the grieving, the longing we have that we have not been able to name.
Our songs will call back the ancestors as well as the gods and the primal giants.

Dagaz And Ingwaz

There is a place in the center of Dagaz where dark turns to light and light turns to dark. This single point in the rune is a liminal or threshold place. Such a place exists on the horizon at the moment the sun rises up. It also exists at spring equinox, the tipping point when the days start to become longer than the nights.

Ingwaz is a rune of fertility, virility, fecundity and potential.
It is all possibility. It is the energy that engorges, building up and releasing at the moment of orgasm. Ingwaz is like a

strand of DNA encoded with genetic information and inherited characteristics. Ingwaz can emerge from the East, generating new life from transformation. Ingwaz can bring us face to face with Ingvi Freyr and his twin sister Freya. They were often ·honored in spring with sacred fertility rites and rituals. Fertility is linked to sexuality.

Sexuality is bound to creativity.

They are both spiritual.

The East Wind

As I am writing this at the end of December, the East Wind is blowing into Portland, Oregon from the Columbia River Gorge. It is intense, cold, scouring. It brings with it the memories and stories of the powerful forces that shaped the Gorge. Earthquakes, ice dams breaking, fires and eruptions and the forces of water lifting huge boulders and carving stone. If I were to travel in the direction of the East Wind I would wind my way up the river, following it until I arrived at the place where it turns and heads North. Then I might meet Kari, the North Wind, who would be bringing something of his own down from British Columbia, Canada into the Gorge.

If East is the direction of beginnings, of emerging, of coming into form, is it possible that the East Wind as ruler of that direction is connected with the power of language and the ability to speak things into existence?

Would that connect the East Wind to Os and Ansuz, and possibly the sound of all the runes as vibrations of creation?

How is the East Wind different in each of the seasons?

What is the nature of the East Wind in Spring compared to how it blows in Winter?

That would depend on your geographical location. Blowing in off the ocean on the East coast of the United States would not be the same as blowing down the Columbia River Gorge. And in Northern Europe, would the East Wind bring information from somewhere in Russia?

Are all the East Winds in various parts of the world, at various times of the year, the offspring of the ancient beings who blew in the beginning alongside Kari?

Who am I?

Where am I?

What time is it?

Which way is the wind blowing?

What do I need?

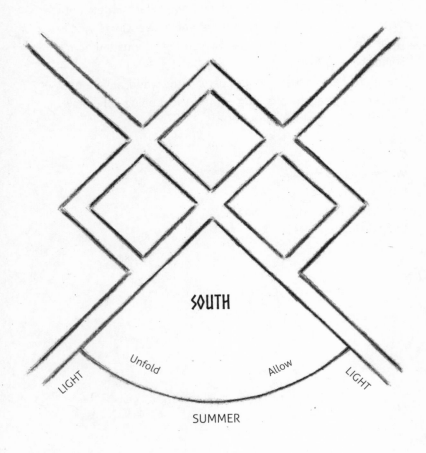

SOUTH

Allow

Unfold

Evolve

Root

Mature

Ripen

THE SOUTH

Step into the Center with your staff.
Step into the middle of your life.
You are not an observer or an outsider.
You are part of all of it.
There is no place to go.
There is no place to be from.
You are already here.
Claim your sovereignty.
You are responsible for your own life and the decisions that
you make.

Ask the questions,

Who am I?
Where am I?
What time is it?
Which way is the wind blowing?
What do I need?

Standing in the Center, which way would you turn to face the
South?
It does not matter.
There is no right way or wrong way.
This is about you.
No one can tell you which way to turn.
Seeking direction from outside authority discourages us from
having our own experiences and trusting our own senses.
When we always look to someone else we are more easily
manipulated, more easily swayed by the ideas of others.

How can someone else know what your life is supposed to look and feel like?

Learn to trust yourself.

You may decide that once you are in the Center you are already facing South so there is no need to turn.

How fast has your life become?

How busy?

Does panic or fear arise with the mere thought of silence, stillness, patience and waiting?

Stepping into the South can provide a reality check.

South is the place of stillness, patience and allowing.

It demands listening, waiting, watching and paying attention.

It is about regaining a sense of timing, a sense of order and embracing a deeper understanding of the natural process and progression of life.

It is the place of the longest day and the shortest night.

It is part of the endless cycle.

Unfold, harvest, transform, emerge.

Follow The Rules

What if you removed the words?

South, West, North, East.

Top, bottom, down, up.

Left and right.

Which direction would you turn if you were seeking wisdom about growing deep roots or ripening or the need for patience as something unfolds in its own time?

The Wheel is a tool.

The directions provide a simple map and give a sense of structure.

But there is danger when we turn them into a rulebook or carve them onto stone.

For example, my heart might be telling me that something is ripening and maturing and I need to turn to the North for wisdom.

My mind might interfere and say I should not do that because North is not the right direction. It said so in the book.

You might decide to turn in all directions.

You might decide to stand still in the Center.

We squander our creative energies and dull our intuition when we believe that we can only do things in a certain way.

Go to the guru.

Listen to the priest.

Follow the rules found in the book.

They are carved in stone like the Ten Commandments.

Perhaps the only thing that is really carved in stone is your epitaph.

Perhaps not.

Find a balance.

Some outside guidance and direction can be helpful but in the end we must learn to trust ourselves, our personal knowing, our own inner wisdom.

Where Am I?

This is an important question. Rune wisdom comes to us from the Motherland of Northern Europe. In order for it to be vibrant and alive it must be relevant. It must be useful in different situations, cultures, climates and times.

For instance, in the Northern hemisphere the sun arcs across the sky to the right. That is not true in the Southern hemisphere. It arcs to the left. Arcing to the right is not the right way. It is one way. Using the Wheel and turning clockwise is not better than turning counterclockwise, nor is one positive and the other negative. There are some popular pagan practices that seem to imply that turning to the right or sunwise is the proper or correct way and that turning to the left is somehow against that, or counter.

Do not do something a certain way just because it is written in a book or because it is marked on the calendar.

Ask questions instead.

Where am I?
What do I see with my own eyes?
What is happening in the sky above me?
What is happening all around me?
What is needed?

Pay attention.

For instance, the month of December is the middle of summer south of the equator. Why would you celebrate Christmas, a winter holiday with reindeer and snow, when what you are experiencing are long, hot summer days and short nights?

Do you celebrate because the calendar says it is Christmas? Or because everyone else is doing it?

Would you celebrate spring fertility rites when the leaves are falling off the trees?

Pay attention to where you are and what time it is.

Are you are sitting under an oak tree waiting for apples?

Patience

The South reminds us that patience is necessary when waiting for something to ripen or mature. If fruit is not ripe, it is not ripe. If it is still green and hard it will be sour or bitter, not pleasant to eat. There is helplessness in the presence of nature. You have to be patient with the timing, orderliness and progression. You have to be still, allowing the natural process to occur and that process is determined by the wisdom inherent in each plant and tree, each fruit and vegetable. And ripening is dependent upon light, water, warmth and soil as well.

South invites us to watch as things unfold, evolve and develop. And the amount of time always varies. If you plant a seedling apple tree in the fall do not expect apples by the end of the following summer. You will be disappointed. It is not going to happen.

You decide to uproot the young apple tree because it is not bearing fruit.
You think there must be something wrong with it.
You go buy another seedling and plant it.
The same thing happens the next summer.
No apples.
You uproot the second one.
You continue to do this year after year.
You will never have apples.
There is nothing wrong with the trees.
It takes an apple tree between five to ten years to produce a good crop. If you are sitting in the shade in summer sipping apple cider you can be sure it did not come from the tree you planted last year.
You cannot hurry the natural cycle.

Nature cannot be rushed nor can it be delayed. This is the wisdom held in Jera.

Berries on the bush ripen quickly on hot summer days. Berries are not apples.

A rabbit's gestation period is 31 days and an elephant's is almost two years. They are both mammals and they are very different. It takes a finch's egg 11 days to hatch but you must wait 35 days for a swan. They are both eggs. They are both birds and they are different.

You can use this wisdom in your own life.
Face the South.
Remember that everything has its own timing, its own rhythm.
Stop looking for what is wrong.
Are you dealing with an oak tree or a berry bush?
In order for an oak tree to start producing acorns it has to reach what is considered full maturity. That can take up to 20 years. Waiting 20 years for an oak tree to grow acorns is a long time. If acorns are your only food source, you will starve to death waiting under a young tree.
Nothing is wrong.
Nothing needs to be fixed.
You may be helpless in the presence of the cycle of the oak tree but you still have choice.
You can decide to wait, you can sit under another tree or you can decide to eat something else.

Ask yourself,

What time is it?
How long will it take for this particular situation to ripen and come to maturity?

It is important to know what time it is because once something is mature it does not continue to mature. When the apple is ripe it falls off the tree and begins to rot.
Unfolding moves into destruction.
It takes patience and intimacy to know when that moment is.
It takes allowing and acceptance as well.

This principle is also true for us as humans.
Once we reach maturity we begin to die.
We may not want to think this way.
It is the truth however.
The turning of the Wheel.
The seasons of the year.
Life and death.
Nothing is ever wasted in nature.
It is an endless cycle of return.

The timing of something is dependent upon circumstances and location. Some things may take hundreds or thousands of years to decompose.
Place them in the path of molten lava or a firestorm and they can be consumed and transformed in an instant.

Jera

Jera is a rune that holds the wisdom of patience. It is right timing in nature, the turning of the Wheel of the seasons. It is a rune that can be explored in all of the directions. Jera is most often connected with harvest and the gathering time. All things ripen and mature at their own pace. We cannot change that. However, we can decide what we want to do and how we wish to interact.

Am I going to let it fall to the ground so the birds and worms eat it?
Do I leave it to rot and nourish the soil?
Am I going to pick it and eat it now?
Am I going to store it so I have something to eat during the winter when nothing is growing?
Should I save it to plant next spring?

Being able to answer such questions takes patience, attention and intimacy with nature. This cannot happen if we are always in a hurry or super busy.
Some people are so addicted to constant stimulation the mere thought of stillness causes them stress.

Nature teaches us all that we need to know about life.
Ask questions. Listen for the answers.

Do I need a forest fire in order for my seeds to sprout?
Am I dealing with a berry bush or an oak tree?
Will this ripen if I pick it while it is still green?
Does the river need to freeze so the fish can survive the winter?

A few years ago I decided to create a handmade book of rune poems using handmade paper. It was to be hand stitched and bound in leather, printed using moveable type that had to be handset and run through a printing press. To do this I hired the services of a local Portland artist, Clare Carpenter of Tiger Food Press. Clare could not produce my book using computer-generated files. She had to go into her studio and set the type, letter by letter, space by space and then run it through the printing press. I had to be willing to be patient with the process.

If I wanted something printed immediately, making a handmade book was not a good choice. I had to allow the process to unfold on its own, literally letter by letter. There was nothing I needed to do nor did I need to intervene to speed things up.

Are you willing to let life unfold at its own pace?
Do you need to intervene?
Should you do something just because you can?
Is it appropriate?
Are you interfering or assisting?
Are you discerning enough to know the difference?
Can you accept that even when you have tended and nurtured something the outcome may not be what you expected or what you wanted?

There is a certain sense of helplessness in nature.
This place of unfolding reminds us that the outcome is not solely dependent upon what we do or do not do. Many other forces and factors are at work over which we have no control.

As you observe the process you can ask yourself,

What is my relationship with waiting for something to ripen or finish?
What are my expectations?
How willing am I to allow?

Below The Surface

Some things mature below the surface, hidden underground in the dark. Root vegetables such as carrots, beets, turnips and rutabagas. If we only look at what is growing above ground in the light, we miss an entire part of earth wisdom.

What is growing and developing in your life, unseen, below the surface?
How will you know when it is time to harvest it?

Dagaz In The South

We live in a culture that expects things to be instant and immediate.
Microwaves. Fast food. Instant hot water.
High-speed internet. Overnight or same-day delivery.
Rapid weight loss. Five-minute porn. Three-second orgasms.
When something does not happen fast enough, we grow impatient and think something must be wrong.

Dagaz reminds us that we need both high speed and snail slow. There must be balance. And as Dagaz shows us by its form, sometimes we must be willing to be neither slow nor fast. We must be the middle where the diagonal lines cross. One is not better than the other, just different.

How do we find our way with what exists?

We do not need to get rid of anything just because it is fast, thinking somehow that we will be better or more spiritual or happier just because we slow down.
What we long for is balance.
There is value in fast.
There is value in slow.

And even in our high-speed world we still appreciate aged cheese, vintage wine, vine-ripened tomatoes and stew that has simmered all day.

When the Wheel is out of balance it wobbles.
When it wobbles, it wears out faster.
So do we.
We have things that have sprouted in the East that we carry into the South to mature.
We have things that have sprouted in the East that we decide not to water and let die instead.
Neither life nor death is good or bad.
They are equal.
They exist side by side.
This is nature.

Working with the wisdom of the Wheel may activate or trigger in you some sense of longing or nostalgia, remembering in your body what it is like to live at a slower pace. Even if you have never done it, you may carry the memory of what it feels like to sit in the cool shade of a tree on a warm summer day listening to bird song.
Skylarks and wrens, waxwings and swallows.
A field of wild flowers vibrant and alive with bees.
White puffy clouds in a sky as blue as a hedge sparrow's egg.

You are not watching television or texting or wearing headphones.
You have no place to go and nothing to do.
You are having the experience of slowness.

When you sit in the shade, in silence, what do you hear?
What do you see?
What do you smell?
How long does it take you to slow down and unfold?

Othila

What is it like to live on the land long enough to know how it
breathes through the seasons of growing, maturing, harvesting
and stillness? Ingwaz and Othila join together, sprouting and
rooting on ancestral homeland. Our indigenous ancestors in the
North were intimate with the land. They were born on it. They
were joined to it. They ate from it, cared for it and were buried
in it. Even when they followed the reindeer as they migrated,
they knew the rhythm of the places they traveled through and
the places they left and returned to.

Living in harmony with the runes reminds us that the land that
feeds us is the land we came from and the land we return to.
When we become the ancestors, our bodies feed the earth so it
can feed the future.

This is the endless cycle of return, the Wheel of life.

Have you ever planted a tree on the land where you live and
stayed long enough to see the tree grow to maturity and
produce?

It is a tradition in some cultures to plant a tree in honor of the
birth of a child. Sometimes the placenta is placed in the ground
with the tree. How intimate it is to be connected to a tree in
such a way. Even if you go wandering or traveling you will
always have a bond with the tree that grows on the land where
you were born.

Have you ever planted a garden and watched it grow and mature? The longer you live on a piece of land the more you come to understand the way the sun moves and the way the wind blows. You know the soil. Each area has its own personality.

What is the landscape of your life?
Is it sloped or flat?
Does it drain well?
Is the ground hard and compacted?
What about the sun and rain?
What kind of garden grows?

Intimacy

Here is a story I heard during my wanderings in Italy.
In the region of Tuscany there is a grove of olive trees behind an old seminary. It was explained to me that each tree grows enough olives to produce about a liter of olive oil. When the olives from a single tree are pressed separately and the oil is bottled, each bottle has a unique and distinctive taste. No matter how subtle it might be, it is different. All the trees are growing side by side in the same grove. One is growing on a bit of a slope. Another is sheltered from the wind. Another has access to more water than the others. Every tree is an individual, just like humans and every bottle of oil is different. As the story goes, there was a farmer who tended the grove. He knew the trees so well he could match each bottle to a specific tree just by tasting the oil.

Such a story could be told about dairy cows as well. The milk from each cow is distinctive and unique, depending on what she ate, where she grazed as well as who she is. We live in a time when everything is mixed together, blended and homogenized. What a gift it is to live so connected to the land and to life that you know by taste which tree produced the oil and which cow gave the milk. Few of us ever get to have such an experience. Such intimacy would alert you if something shifted with the land or the cow or the weather or the availability of water and you would know when it was time to take action or when it was time to move on.

Even if you live in an apartment in the middle of a large city, you can turn in the direction of the South, connect with your indigenous ancestors and remember through them what it was like to know the land.
Even if all you have is a potted plant on a windowsill or a balcony you can still ask the ancestors to teach you how to use their wisdom in the life you are living right now.
Pay attention to things differently.
The earth is our home.
All life comes from the land.

Stand in the Center.
Turn and face the South.
Learn about the patience needed for things to grow and the willingness to allow that to happen.

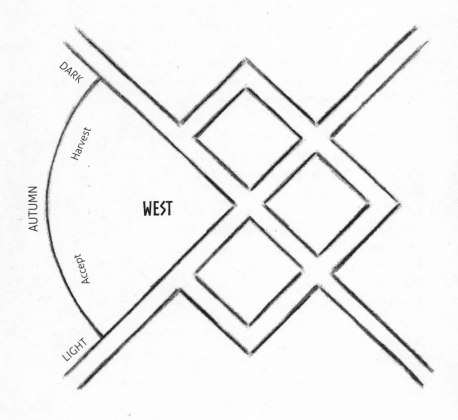

WEST

Accept

Harvest

Discern

Disappear

Destroy

THE WEST

Step into the Center.
Always begin in the Center.
You are encircled by the horizon, that edge place where things
appear and disappear, the place you can never reach because it
moves with you as you move.
Ask the questions,

Who am I?
Where am I?
What time is it?
Which way is the wind blowing?
What do I need?

The answers are always different.
There are no right answers.

In the Center you become the Tree. Your roots grow down
and deep, tapping into the dark, hidden places where they
find nourishment and water. They anchor you to the earth,
your home. Your branches grow up and out, calling to the sun
and wind. Your trunk holds movement in stillness. Energy
flows down and up. You are the past, existing in the present,
remembering your future.

Face The Setting Sun

Standing in the Center, which way would you turn to face the
sun as it disappears?
The place where light hides.

The place where the ancestors go when they return to the earth.
The place of harvest.
The home of death and endings.
Life comes from death at harvest.
Disappear, transform, emerge, unfold.
This is the Wheel of Life.

We live on the earth.
It is our home.
We orient ourselves in relationship to the sun.
Where does it appear?
Where does it disappear?
Which way does it arc across the sky?

The rising and setting of the sun have been experienced by all people throughout all time. This is constant. The variations are based on seasons and locations. If you live near or above the Arctic Circle, there are times when the sun hovers low along the horizon. In the northernmost inhabited regions of Europe, the sun rises only once in summer and sets only once in winter. It stays light all through the summer giving rise to the name Land of the Midnight Sun. In winter the sun stays hidden so it is dark all day and all night. We call this phenomenon Polar Night.

Our native Northern European ancestors lived with these extremes. The appearance and disappearance of the sun had a rhythm unique to their location and their survival depended upon awareness, understanding and acceptance of this rhythm.

Turn and face the direction of the disappearing sun and ask the questions,

Where am I?
What am I seeing?
What happens for me when I watch the sun go down?
Does it drop into the earth or the ocean or disappear behind a mountain?
How am I experiencing my life at this particular moment?
Is the darkness rising up behind me?

If you live inland, you may see the sun disappear into the earth or into a mountain. If you live on the western edge of a continent, you might see the sun disappear into the ocean. I live in Portland, Oregon. I see the setting sun drop behind the hills to the West and as it does it illuminates a large skyscraper that dominates the Portland skyline, turning it pink as the light changes.

Even though I live in a city I can still turn and face the direction of the setting sun. The reality of my life is different from the life of someone who lives in the forest or out on the open plains and I am part of nature no matter how much I am surrounded by concrete and metal, freeways and airports.

In spite of what we have been told by science and technology, the sun disappears when it sets.
That is what we see, observe, and experience.
And the rising sun emerges out of the water or out of the land. It returns from the place beyond the horizon where it disappeared, trading places in its cycle with the dark.

Your Own Experience

Most of our ancestors did not travel very far from home. There were a few wanderers who walked the land or got on ships and went exploring. Some were scattered far and wide due to famine, disease, climate change or natural disasters but in general, most people lived their entire life in a relatively small area. It was possible for people to live and die and never see the ocean or a mountain or a forest. Location determined what they experienced and language developed around those experiences. What they experienced also determined how they related to life.

Perhaps this is hard for us to grasp. Today we are able to travel with ease and speed to any location on the globe. This is a relatively recent phenomenon. We also have access, through television, the Internet and books, to images of places we have heard about but never traveled to.

Does wisdom come only from experience or from the knowledge and information as well?

I grew up in California, a state with a very long coastline. I was often at the beach and when I watched the sun set it dropped down into the Pacific Ocean. When my family moved for a short time to Wyoming it seemed strange to me to meet people who had seen pictures of the ocean but had never traveled there. They had never had the experience of dipping their toes into the great salt water.

Once, while teaching a class, I asked the students to share their experiences of sunset. One man commented that he gets nostalgic and loves the amazing colors that appear in the sky. Another said, "*when the sun begins to set I get all excited. I get creative and I know that the rest of the world around me is beginning to shut down. I don't feel so bombarded.*"

Kristie shared, "*From my home I can't actually see the sun set but I know it's time when I see the crows flying west. That's when my real day starts.*"

Margrethe called sunset a transition time, a time when things begin to get quiet. She stated, "*I start to unwind and shut down because I go to bed early and I prepare for dream time.*"

For Clare sunset is a time of day when she is able to open herself up and be more receptive. "*Being receptive for me is a bit different from being creative. The creative part happens for me later on in the night.*"

One person gets more creative. Another prepares to sleep and dream while others are more receptive and nostalgic. Five different people. Five different experiences, each one unique to the person who is having it. The common thread is the setting sun.

What happens for you when the crows begin to fly west and you face the direction of disappearing and death?

As you watch the light disappear, do you ever pay attention to the dark that is rising up behind you?

Do you become more active?

Is this a time of enhanced receptivity?

It could be a time of enhanced creativity if your creative self is nourished and fed by stillness and darkness.

Edge Places

West is an edge place, a place of transition. It is a time of shift, a shift that slows life down as the dark returns. There is no way to ignore this. Things happen when we slow down and rest, things that cannot happen when we are busy and fast.

As the sun leaves, darkness arrives, and things happen in the dark that do not happen in the light. Not bad things. Not negative things. Nothing is wrong and nothing needs to be fixed. Darkness is rich and valuable, necessary and welcomed. This is the time during the cycle when we begin to see the stars. Stars disappear at sunrise and appear again at sunset. The light hides things from us. The darker it becomes, the more we are able to see.

Our native Northern European ancestors embraced and valued times of darkness, spending long periods of time observing the night sky and paying attention. How else would they have been able to build with such accuracy the enormous structures and stone circles that are still in perfect alignment with the movement of the stars?

The rhythmic cycle of the Wheel applies to the movement between dark and light. It applies to the changing of the seasons, from summer into autumn, into winter, into spring. It applies to the birth of something that unfolds and matures, goes to seed, dies and rots, so it can transform into what is next.

Return to the Tree.
The energy gathered by the leaves from the sun travels down
the trunk into the roots that grow below the surface, beneath
our feet. Whether it is the darkness of night or the darkness of
winter, the energy of a tree goes down into the roots.

Paying attention to what is happening around you contributes
to balance and wellbeing. West is a good direction to face
when you are ready to get out of your head and set aside the
high vibrations that surround you in daily life. The world of
technology, texting and traffic, high speed and headphones.
Just like a tree, you get fed, watered, nourished and rested
when you drop down into the earth, into the low vibrations
below the surface.

Stars

As the light disappears and the dark returns, we begin to see
the stars. They are overhead all the time, just not visible in the
light. It is important for us to remember and appreciate that
some things can only be seen when it is dark. A vast number of
people living on earth at this time have never experienced total
darkness.
We currently suffer from global light pollution.

Have you ever considered light to be a form of pollution?
Do we suffer from spiritual light pollution as well?
What is hidden to us when there is too much light?
What do we lose when we never allow ourselves to experience
the dark?

What are we missing when we no longer consider darkness as valuable?
What do we miss spiritually when we are focused only on the light?

Without total darkness we miss the true magnificence of the night sky.
The ancestors did not think of the stars as being really far away. For them the stars were present, very close and there were countless numbers of them in different colors, sizes and varying degrees of brightness, all twinkling and blinking. They did not think the stars were bigger than the sun. That is not what they saw or experienced. The sun was enormous, powerful, and awe-inspiring. The stars were small.

We believe what we believe because of what we have been taught and because we have been told that those who are teaching such things are authorities and experts. What we have been taught to believe now is just as true as what our ancestors believed. We can value and appreciate what we learn from science and we can value and appreciate what we personally experience. Humans have fantastic imaginations. We are able to make the night sky whatever we want it to be and all of it is true and none of it is true. Each of us gets to define it, describe it, experience it and make it mean anything. This is the part that so often gets forgotten.

The sun disappears and the dark returns and as it does it brings with itself, from beyond the horizon, the stars. And throughout time, humans have seen patterns, shapes and images in clustered groups and they have named these groups as well as named the individual stars. They saw wagons and bears, swans and dragons, club-carrying giants wearing belts and cows with milk spilling from their udders.

Returning to the Center and the Tree, we are reminded of the connections that exist between what is seen above and what exists below. It is quite likely that some of the lost teachings yet to be uncovered include the wisdom and understanding our ancestors had regarding the sky lines that connect the stars and the ley lines or dragon lines that connect power points on the earth.

Could it be that there are certain times when patterns of star lines align with patterns of earth lines?
And could it be that when this happens, an activation or energizing occurs?

These energy lines all around the globe could be likened to acupuncture meridians. The sky mirrors points on the earth and the earth mirrors points in the sky. This is the pattern of the Tree, the branches and roots mirroring each other.

Walking The Energy Lines

There was a time when great herds of reindeer crisscrossed Europe, all the way down to the Alps. When reindeer migrate, they walk the energy lines of the earth, following ancient paths to food and safety. These lines connect with star lines above us in the heavens. We benefit when we find energy lines and walk them. We can do this even in a city. The earth benefits.

The stars benefit. The reindeer benefit. This connection is symbiotic. This may be why there is a resurgence of interest in pilgrimage paths. It is the activation, not the destination. The path of pilgrims today is often tightly woven into Church imagery yet we know that long before the coming of Christianity people walked the earth's energy lines, following the reindeer. There are many clues left behind that support this. One such clue is the full name given to the currently popular Camino. El Camino de Santiago de Compostela. The Road of St. James of the Field of Stars. There are numerous historical references to the connection between ley lines, earth paths and stars, and of course, these connections are more ancient than the Church.

Is the resurgence of interest in walking these paths because the earth needs to be reactivated, or because we need to be reconnected? Or both?

Constellations And The Nine Worlds

I am outside. The sun is disappearing behind me in the West. I am facing East, the rising up of the dark. The sky is opening and I begin to see the constellations.
I remember I am in the Center of the universe. All things extend away from me in all directions. Below, above, inside and beyond. I am also in the Center of all Nine Worlds.

Imagine what it would mean if the rising constellations are the different worlds within the Tree.
This is possible.

Instead of referring to the signs of the zodiac as brought
to us from the Middle East, what if we spoke of the rising
constellations in the language of the Nine Worlds?

The sign of Niflheim.
The sign of Muspelheim.
The sign of Jotunheim.

If you were born at the time that Muspelheim was present in
the sky, are you a descendent of Surt or Logi, giants from the
realm of fire?
Instead of saying you are a Pisces or an Aries, could you say you
are from Svartalfheim and you carry the characteristics of that
realm?

We all come from the Tree, which exists in the Void. We are
all connected in this way to the Nine Worlds. Some of us are
descendents of the frost giants and some of us from the fire
giants. Some of us carry in our blood hints of the Alfar, also
known as Elves or characteristics of the dwarves, the Duergar.
This could be true, or not. It seems to be worth exploring.

Is it any more difficult or far-fetched to believe this about the
stars and the Nine Worlds than it is to believe in the validity of
the creatures of currently popular horoscopes?
What if the place you go to when you die is actually
determined by which one of the Nine Worlds is present in the
sky at the time of your death?

That would give a different perspective to the concept of reincarnation or return. That would mean that when you come back you return from the realm you went into at your death. It would have nothing to do with how good or how bad you were during your life and it would have nothing to do with working out your past karma. It would instead relate to the connection that existed between the sky above and earth below at the time of your death and the time of your birth.

What if memories of this ancient wisdom from the North are activated when we face the rising up of the dark instead of the rising up of the light?

It is written that the Nine Worlds are in the roots of the Tree, in the dark. We cannot see them beneath our feet but we can see them mirrored in the stars when the light leaves. We look up to see how we are sourced from below. The stars create the map for us to find our way down so we can navigate the roots and the Nine Worlds.

West is the place of the ancestors, the place they disappear. West holds wisdom just like seeds and grains store the knowledge of life, preserving it through Winter so it can emerge again in Spring.

Is that why the West wind is called both destroyer and preserver by Percy Shelley as he writes in his poem, "Ode to the West Wind"?

Nidhogg In The Roots

Beneath our feet the dragon serpent dwells. There are some who believe she is damaging or destroying the Tree by constantly gnawing on the roots. Perhaps these are the same ones who believe that only negative, evil, and bad things happen in the dark, down below.

The destruction that happens below the surface, in the moist, dark places of the earth is necessary. Things are eaten underground and transformed so something new and vital can emerge. The same thing happens on a larger scale in the universe. She consumes herself, expands and then contracts. This cycle is expressed in the imagery of the Tree. The dragon gnawing, the leaves dripping, and the Nornir tending. This is also embodied in the World Serpent Jormungund, as symbolized in the ouroboros, the serpent consuming and feeding itself at the same time.

What happens when you become the Tree in the Center?
What moves up and down in your life?
What rots and is consumed below the surface so something new can appear?

Discernment

Our indigenous ancestors knew the sky and the stars. They watched the sky because it had much to teach them about the energy on earth. When we sit in the dark it connects us to the roots. Most likely this is the truth about the squirrel Ratatoskr who scurries up and down the trunk of the World Tree. She is not causing mischief. She is showing us the way to connect what is above with what is below, embracing both as necessary and vital.

Where in your life do you need to connect what is beneath your feet with what is beyond the horizon?

West is the place of discernment. Discernment is the ability to separate and divide things, to be able to distinguish one thing from another. In order to sort anything you must first be able to recognize the differences.

West can connect us with the time of year we call Autumn, the time of harvest, of gathering in, of dying.
Autumn is not the time of year to till the soil and plant.
It is not the time of year when things are taking root and growing to maturity.
Things are dying.
Leaves are falling off the trees.
In Autumn we pay attention and decide.
The Wheel is turning.

What and how much do we need to gather in so we can survive the coming Winter?
What needs to be left in the field?

West is a powerful direction to turn when you are seeking wisdom regarding a decision that demands discernment. Easy access to abundance of all kinds of food at all times of the year has distanced modern day humans from this aspect of survival.

Autumn equinox marks the time of equal dark and equal light. Our ancestors were well aware that from the equinox on, the days would shorten and the nights would get longer until they reached Winter Solstice, the longest night of the year. They marked the equinox with celebrations and at the same time they had to take stock.

Had they gathered in enough fuel to last until Spring?
Had they stored enough food to feed themselves through the dark of Winter?
Could they survive until things began to sprout again and birds started laying their eggs?

Not only would they take stock at harvest, they would do so again at Winter Solstice and then again around February 1 which was the halfway point between solstice and Spring Equinox. Their survival through the Winter was dependent upon how they paid attention in the Autumn.

Would you do things differently in the Autumn if life and death hung in the balance based on the choices you make?

Several years ago at Summer Solstice, I was visiting Saltoluokta, a place in the north of Sweden above the Arctic Circle. The winter had been extra long and the birch trees were just beginning to leaf even though it was mid-June. The Sami woman I was staying with explained that in times past her people depended on the birch leaves, eating them like salad, a Scandinavian version of spring greens. And if spring was long in coming, they would still be depending on the reindeer they had killed in the Autumn, not just the meat but the contents of the intestines as well. Their survival was linked not only to how much attention they had paid to what they gathered in but also to how they had rationed it out.

This wisdom is found in the West. It is also a reality check on why it was not possible to be a vegetarian in the Far North and certainly not a vegan.

Who am I?
Where am I?
What time is it?
What do I need?
Which way is the wind blowing?

Ancestors

We might choose to face the setting sun as a way to connect with our ancestors. When they died we put them into the ground. We buried them in the mound, the grave or a cave. Even if we sent them out to sea, they disappeared just like the sun. And if we burned them, eventually their ashes returned to the earth.

Do our ancestors live in the West, in the place of disappearing? Are they the seeds, the nuts, the acorns that hold the memory and information necessary for new life to sprout and grow? When the Wheel turns, do they move to the North to be transformed?

Wisdom

T.S. Eliot, poet, essayist and social critic, asked,
"Where is the wisdom we have lost in knowledge? Where is the knowledge we have lost in information?"

Stand in the Center.
Face the West.
Step into the stillness that connects us to the wisdom gained from reflection and discernment.

Wisdom does not come from information nor do we gain it simply from knowledge. Wisdom is sourced from the silence and the darkness, the times of quiet contemplation where we gain perspective.
Sit in the West and watch the sun go down.
Follow it until you find your ancestors.
They know more than you know because they have gone before.

The West Wind

A wind is blowing in from the West. If you lived on a western coast in close proximity to the ocean, it could carry in the smell of the sea, the sea weed and salt water. In some ancient cultures, the West Wind was considered female and was connected to gentle things and music. Our ancestors did not read a book to find out what the wind meant. How they felt about the winds, what names they used to speak of them and what they believed were all based upon their observations and experiences. I have not been able to find anything written about the West Wind in Norse mythology. I need to form my own relationship based on my own experiences. In order for any of us to form such relationships, we need to spend time outdoors feeling the wind blowing from the West or from any direction for that matter. The intimacy necessary for naming is based on experience and paying attention.

When the West Wind blows how do you feel?
Does it blow in from the ocean, the desert, the mountains?
Is the West Wind male or female, or neither, or both?
What is it like in each of the seasons?

I have lived in many different places both in Europe and the United States. When I think of the West Wind, I think of autumn and I smell warm, spiced cider and apples that are bruised by falling to the ground and bees buzzing and ants crawling. The West Wind reminds me of new mown hay and piles of fallen leaves smoldering in the orchard. Sometimes when it blows I can hear the old songs my ancestors sang as they gathered wood for winter or harvested a crop.

Does the West Wind carry songs of thanksgiving or songs of mourning?
Listen.
What songs do you hear?
What do you know when the West Wind blows?

Stand in the Center.
Turn and face the West.

Watch the sun as it disappears and ask,

How do I feel?
What do I hear?
What do I smell?
What do I remember?
What practice or ritual do I do each day that connects me with the return of the dark?
Do I feel differently when I see the sun disappearing into the water compared to disappearing into the earth?
Where does the light go?
Does it disappear into the dark?
Does the dark appear from within the light?
How would my life be different if my day began at sunset?
Would I live in another way?

Transitions

West is the end of a day, the end of a season, the end of anything. It is a place of transition. There is no rush. There is no delay. West joins together with the South in reminding us of the natural timing and rhythm of all things.

Something is ending in your life.
A job. A relationship. A role you have played. A belief you have held.
Whenever something ends, something new begins.
Take it into the West.
Take time to sort and differentiate.
Use discernment.
Be still.

Pay attention.
Do not be impatient with the process.
Ask yourself questions,

What did I learn?
What did I gain?
How did I maintain what is now ending?
What part am I playing in the destruction?
What part am I playing in what is beginning?
Do I ever want to have such an experience again?

Go back to the teachings of the Wheel.
Something emerged in the Spring, unfolded and matured in the Summer and is now finishing in Autumn.
You must decide if you are going to leave it in the field or if you are going to gather it in.
You must decide how much of it you will eat now and how much you will save to eat later to sustain yourself through the long, dark, cold months of Winter.
You get to decide how much you will store to plant come Spring.
Or, if you do not like what grew, you may decide to never plant it again.

How can you use the wisdom of the West in day-to-day life?

Remember, discernment is about sorting. Take time each day to sort through your experiences. Take time to sort through things whenever something ends. When something ends, something new always begins. If you move too quickly into what is next, you miss the opportunity to gain wisdom from the experience. There is value in the in-between times, the dawn and dusk of life. When we do not give ourselves time to experience the experience, we find ourselves repeating the same things over and over again. We take the same problem or issue into the next job, the next relationship, the next move because we did not sort. It takes time to know what to do with what happened.

Whenever something ends, take the time to go down into your roots, below the surface. Take time to go inside. Remember that we are fed and nourished from below. Our roots anchor us to the earth, providing balance and stability.
There are some who think that this is shadow work.
It is not.
A shadow is cast when there is light.
This is root work.
Roots grow in the dark. There is no light in the dark. Dark is dark. It is filled with great and wondrous things. It is a source of wisdom.

Destroyer And Preserver

Percy Shelley, an English Romantic poet, wrote a poem called "Ode to the West Wind." You might want to read his poem and ponder it. Feel your way in. Here is a brief excerpt.

O wild West Wind, thou breath of Autumn's being,
Thou, from whose unseen presence the leaves dead
Are driven, like ghosts from an enchanter fleeing...
Wild Spirit, which art moving everywhere;
Destroyer and Preserver...

Like withered leaves to quicken a new birth!
And, by the incantation of this verse,
Scatter, as from an unextinguished hearth
Ashes and sparks...
O Wind,
If Winter comes, can Spring be far behind?

The poet spoke of the West Wind as both a destroyer and a preserver.

It blows the dead leaves off the trees, but it also scatters the seeds that will bring new life in Spring.

Even though we are going into the dark, we need not fear the coming Winter because its arrival assures us that Spring is not far behind.

This is the Circle.

This is the Wheel.

Pay Attention

There is a truth about harvest that is timeless and global.

If you plant oats, oats are going to grow.

You are not going to get tomatoes.

There is something sobering and yet simple in knowing this. The things that start showing up in your life may not always be what you want. Sometimes things are growing because they blew in with the wind. But you must remember that what you plant is what will grow. The West can remind you that you need to pay close attention to your actions.

Harvest in Autumn demands discernment.

You are going into the dark, going into Winter.

What do you need to gather in and how much?
What can you enjoy immediately, perhaps in a feast or celebration?
What must you leave in the field?
What must you save to plant in the coming year?
What are you willing to offer up or hold back?
If you only produce and consume, never giving back, there will be nothing to generate in Spring.

The wisdom of the West can be applied to daily life.
You cannot eat everything through the Winter.
You must trust, be willing to save some seeds and grain to plant come Spring. You are participating in a cycle of survival and continuance.
The land needs to rest without planting. Crops need to be left in the field so organic material can decompose and return nutrients to the soil.
If we do not pay attention to such things, the land becomes dead, the soil gray and lifeless.
Discernment at harvest is determining how much needs to be collected and how much needs to be left so it can return to the earth.
Discernment is knowing how much needs to be saved so there is something left to plant again.
Many of us in the Western world live in places where we can go to mega stores and buy excessive and obscene amounts of food in large containers and multi-packs, justifying our actions with the belief that we are saving money. Sadly, many of the things we buy spoil or go past their freshness dates before we can consume them.

Do we buy based on fear of lack or have we truly taken stock of what we need?

What part do you play in waste and depletion, buying more than you need, or hoarding and storing things you no longer use?

What happens for you in the West?

Several people have said that when they turn in that direction they become really aware of transitions. Others say that the West invites them to leave their windows open in the evening so they can watch the curtains dance.

The West can be a place where you reclaim your heritage, reconnect with your ancestors and experience the completion of the full cycle of inherited grief.

The West can invite you to consider your own death and the part you will play in the cycle of return.

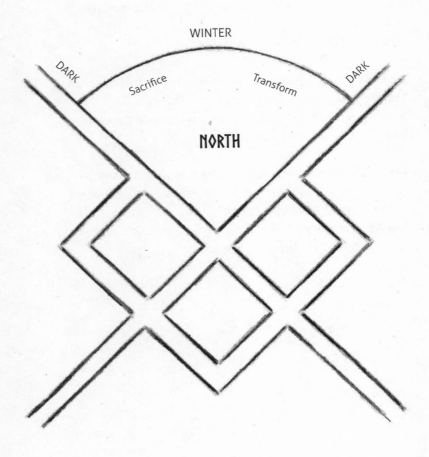

NORTH

Sacrifice

Transform

Initiate

Offer

Complete

THE NORTH

It is dark.
It is cold.
It is Winter.
In the Northern hemisphere it is a time of silence and stillness,
the longest night and the shortest day.
Winter Solstice.
The earth rests.
It is the place of transformation, in between death in Autumn
and emerging in Spring.
It is the time of endings that are also beginnings.

Alignment and sovereignty in the Center.
Anticipation in the East.
Allowing in the South.
Acceptance in the West.
Now we have arrived in the North.
Sacrifice.
The place of helplessness and surrender, of initiation,
completion, and transformation.

What do you feel when you hear these words?
Where do you feel it?
How comfortable are you with helpless and surrender?
What have you completed in your life?
How does it feel to reach completion?
Have you ever made an offering?
Have you ever offered up a sacrifice?
Are they the same or are they different?

Take up your staff.
Step into the Center.
Turn and face the North.

Which way did you turn?
What did you bring with you into the North that you are willing
to offer up in order to continue?
What sacrifices are you willing to make in order to have
something new or different come into your life?

I often hear people talking about making resolutions, setting
intentions for the coming year or aiming for a goal. Rarely do
I hear them speak about what they are willing to offer up or
sacrifice in order to realize what they are seeking.
Feelings of constriction or deprivation often swirl around the
word sacrifice rather than a sense of willingness.
Yet something must always be offered up or released in order
for something else to come into form.
Change brings the death that is necessary for transformation.
The North asks us to examine our willingness to die.

How comfortable are we with old age and death?
How comfortable are we just talking about it?

We are all consumers.
We eat.
We drink.
We consume in order to stay alive and when it is time, we too
will be consumed.

North reminds us that once we are ripe we do not continue to ripen. Once we mature, we go to seed, we drop from the tree, we become a dandelion puff that waits for the wind.
The Wheel turns and we enter the place of dying that leads to sacrifice and initiation.

Ask questions,

What in my life has died?
What in my life is dying?
What in my life needs to die?
What in my life is ready to die?
What am I willing to offer up?
What must I offer up in order to continue?

These questions may not be comfortable, yet they beg to be asked in the North.

We are all part of nature and we are all part of life.
We are made from elements and energy that are continuously being recycled and reused. We are drinking the same water that the builders of Stonehenge used to wash their clothing.
We are a new configuration just as much as we are part of the continuation.

So when you ask, what am I willing to offer up in order to continue, what are you actually saying?
Am I willing to go to seed?
Am I willing to rot?
Am I willing to float in the air and replant someplace else?
Am I willing to die?

That is continuation.

When an offering is made, something is dying and the very act is about survival and continuation.

Nothing comes from nothing.

This brings us back to the questions asked earlier in the book,

When did you enter the story?
Where did you enter the story?

It Is The Cycle

It is the North and the Center and it is the Wheel and all the directions.

North holds the energy of coming to a place in life where you know that what you have been doing and how you have been doing it no longer fits or no longer serves.

It does not feed you.

It does not satisfy you.

You have come to the place of helplessness, surrender and completion.

It can be a job or a business.

It can be a relationship or a partner.

It can be a home or a journey.

It can be a story you have been telling yourself about who you think you are.

It can be a belief system, a spiritual practice or a religion.

It can be anything that no longer works.

In the classes I teach, I often mention my grandfather, Curly Kincaid, a rough old man born in Oklahoma. He had a saying that has served me well and that seems to apply to all sorts of situations,

When the horse dies, get off.

It is a simple and practical statement that carries great insight. Yet, instead of getting off the dead horse, we often try to justify keeping it and dragging it around by saying things such as,

Do you know how much money I paid for this horse?
Do you know how long we have been together?
Do you know how many miles we have ridden?
Do you have any idea what a good friend this horse has been and how much it means to me?
Maybe it's not even dead.
Maybe I just think it's dead.
Maybe it's my fault because I haven't tried hard enough.
I think I will try to give it some vitamins, take it to therapy, encourage it to do yoga . . .

Face the North with your staff in hand.
Something is not working anymore.
Something no longer fits.
The form has changed.
It is finished.
It is complete.
The horse has died.
It can take a lot of courage to look at such things.
It takes discernment, sorting and truth telling.
You can bring these elements into the North from the West.

Consider for instance marriage and intimate relationships.
Is it possible to tell the truth and remain friends?
Do we have to create a situation where we turn the other
person into an enemy so we can justify ending it?
Do we need to create some kind of drama, trauma, and chaos
fueled by anger?
Are we afraid or unwilling to tell the truth, first to ourselves and
then to the other person?

This no longer works.
This is finished.
This is worn out.
The form of this relationship needs to change.

The pair of shoes you love, paid a lot of money for, walked a
thousand miles in, have holes in the soles and they cannot be
repaired.
Rocks get in.
They hurt your feet.
You need to stop wearing them and let them go.
But instead you say, "*I think I will just toughen up, suffer, and
wear them anyway.*"

What no longer serves you?
What no longer satisfies or feeds you?
What no longer works?
Has the horse died?

Use the wisdom of the West to discern these things.
Step into the Center, reclaim your sovereignty and then face
the North.

Sit in the dark.
Sit in the stillness.
Sit in the silence and then offer it up.

If you want something new in your life, if you want something
different, you cannot continue to make the same choices,
engage in the same behaviors, and act in the same way
and expect something to change.

Willingness

To choose is the sacrifice.
Am I willing to change?
Am I willing to do something new or different?

Life is not about something being done to you.
It is participatory.
When you are ready to change, there must be an offering.
Change cannot happen without letting go or without giving
back.
These cycles do not happen just once in your life. They happen
over and over again, when you are 20 or 30 or 55 or 70. It does
not matter. We pass through all of the seasons over and over
again. There may be nostalgia and sadness or even grief but do
not get caught in the past.

What a plant needs in the spring when it has just sprouted is
not going to serve it in the autumn. If you planted a sapling you
may need to place bands around it and anchor it to a stake so
it can deeply root and grow straight. But if you do not take the
bands off they will eventually kill the tree.

This is rune wisdom.

The things that support you at one time can kill you at another time.

The sun that gives you light can also blind you. Sowelo.

The water that sustains your life can also drown you. Laguz.

The fire you need to survive will also destroy you. Nauthiz.

The mother who gave birth may also eat her young. Berkana.

This is the truth of nature and this is the truth for humans because we are not different. We are part of nature and we are nature.

The question "what time is it?" connects us with the question "what do I need?"

I do not need training wheels on my bicycle once I have learned to ride without them.

Sometimes we have to be willing to give up an identity. Maybe we have a career that we trained for in college and it holds meaning for us. We have letters behind our name. We have a certain position in life. We are respected and known. And now we are finished. It is time to retire. We are done.

Sometimes we need to burn our house down and walk away.

Sometimes we must forget who we used to be so we can claim who we are becoming.

This could be Eihwaz, life and death.

This could be Hagalaz, the hailstorm.

This could be Thurisaz, painful chaos.

This could be Yr, the bow and arrow we use to kill so we can eat.

Which Way Is Up?

Looking at the drawing of the Wheel, the Circle overlaid with Gar, the direction shown as North is situated at the top of the page. Why?

Is it because we have been taught that North is at the top?

Is that true?

When you stand in the Center of the Wheel, which way is North?

What feels right to you?

Asking such a question about the North or any direction for that matter provides opportunity to explore alternate perspectives, perhaps new ways to speak about and experience the horizon and the directions.

If you live in the Northern Hemisphere, facing North means you are facing the direction of the nearest polar ice cap, the Arctic, named after the circumpolar constellation Ursa Major, Arktos, the bear. Facing the Arctic, the sun would rise up on your right and arc across the sky to your right. Those of us who live north of the equator refer to this movement as clockwise. However, if you live in the Southern Hemisphere you would face the opposite direction in order to face the nearest polar ice cap, Antarctica, a world that means "opposite to the arctic." The sun would then rise up on your left side and arc across the sky to your left. People in the Northern Hemisphere call this movement to the left counterclockwise. The question is, counter to whom? Counter to what? Counter to the North?

Who decided to put the North at the top of the map and when?

Exploring such questions about opposites reminds us that how we experience and speak about life is in relationship to who we are, what we have been taught and the words used to teach us. And what is at the top has more to do with who drew the maps and who were the conquerors than it does with our location.

Dark And Cold

The West supports us through the transition of the light leaving and the dark returning.
The North is dark.
Some things can only be seen in the dark.
Stars for instance.
The dark reveals the existence of an entire experience that is above us, an experience we can only see it when it is dark. The dark is not bad or evil, something to be feared or something that is less desirable than light.
The dark is its own being.

How do you view the dark?
How do you go into the dark?
How do you use the dark?
Do you think of it in negative terms, as something bad, something to be avoided?
Do you speak of it as if it is less than light or even the absence of light?
What happens when you experience the dark as being at the top?
Would such a view turn the World Tree upside down?
Roots above.
Branches below.

Does the North take you back to the Eihwaz rune and the yew tree? The branches grow down into the earth and become roots, sending up a new tree from the center of the rotted-out trunk. Is there any place in your life where this is happening?

The North is cold and ice.
We can see things, know things and understand things in the cold that we cannot experience when it is warm.
Ice acts as a preservative.
It slows things down.
Sometimes we have experiences or gain information or have ideas that we cannot process quickly. We need a place to keep them. We need more time or another piece to complete the puzzle. Bringing such experiences with you into the North affords a hiding place, a holding place, a place to process. We can put them on ice and wait and when the ice melts, as it always does, the things that have been frozen, slowed down and stilled can now be understood or utilized.
Ice also creates a bridge, a way to cross over water that previously was flowing. Cold turns the water from liquid into solid. You can use the energies of the North to create a way to pass from one place to another.

Equal Exchange

Gebo is often called the gift rune. It is associated with the concept of relationships and partnerships, contracts and agreements. Part of its essence is the energy of equal exchange or reciprocity. Something is given in exchange for something else. In the North, Gebo aligns with the necessity of offerings and sacrifices. Life is a repeat of cycles, over and over again.

Yet nothing is ever the same.

The oak tree produces hundreds of acorns. They fall from
the tree.
Does the tree release them or do they let go when they are
ready?
The acorn holds the future as well as the past.
Disconnected, the acorn ceases to be part of the tree that gave
it life. It becomes its own unique being. It contains within itself
the potential and ability to become another oak tree.
It cannot grow into anything else.
The tree makes an offering.
The acorn makes an offering.
Something ends so something new can begin. Life comes from
life but only through the experience of something dying. We
can only sustain life by consuming things that were once alive.
This is the truth of equal exchange and Gebo.
Equal exchange is the death of something so birth can occur.

Sacrifice

For some people a sacrifice is an offering made to the gods or
the ancestors, as an act of worship or propitiation. Worship is
a word most of us find familiar but what about propitiation?
Propitiation implies appeasing someone or bringing someone
or something to a state of calm. It is a word often used to
describe an offering that is made to a god who is angry or
jealous. But not all offerings and sacrifices are about the gods.

The word sacrifice finds its roots in Latin. It means to make
something sacred or to do something sacred. It can refer to

something being highly valued and important or deserving of great respect.

A sacrifice can be a libation, the pouring out of something.
It can be the offering of something bloodless such as food or objects.
It can be the blood of an animal or even a human.
It usually involves some sort of ritual.

The practice of sacrifice, human as well as animal, is evident in some of the oldest archaeological findings. This should not be shocking to us. Sacred Jewish texts include detailed descriptions and rules regarding animal sacrifices to honor and appease their god. And there are hints in these texts that point to the practice of human sacrifice such as the stories of Abraham and Isaac and the daughter of Jephthah.
And Christianity is a religion based on a human sacrifice that was needed to appease the anger of their god.

Since many people today do not practice any sort of religious ritual that involves blood sacrifices, the terms "doing without" or 'giving something up' may be more familiar.

What might you do without or give up in the North?
How would that lead you to completion and initiation?
What might you offer up to bring something to a state of calm?
What are your thoughts on the matter of sacrifice?
Why did the ancients practice sacrifice?
What purpose did it serve?
How could the essence or principle of it be of value in your life?
What if the sacrifice that is being required in the North is the willingness to die so transformation can occur?
How might this affect your attitude toward growing old?

When Gebo appears in the North it can carry the reminder that when life gives us a gift, we are always required to give something in return or in exchange.

What gift or ability do you have that has been given to you?
How are you using it as an offering or a sacrifice?
Is it possible that the gift we all have been given is the same?
The gift of life which encompasses our creativity, our sexuality and our spirituality?
What if the sacrifice is letting go of old beliefs about what is sacred and what is not?

Sacred And Profane

The word sacrifice comes from Latin and means to make something sacred.
The word profane also comes from Latin and means outside the temple or not sacred.

What if there is no separation between the sacred and the profane?
What if it is not possible to be outside the temple?
If everything is holy there is no need to make something holy.
There would no longer be a need for us to use expressions such as divine feminine or sacred masculine, or holy water or even profanity.

Is killing profane?
The Christian god kills.
Does that mean he is outside the temple?
What if we stop believing that the gods exist on some special, spiritual plane?

What if we stop believing that we are less than they are and in need of salvation?

What if this beautiful, amazing earth is sacred and profane? Then it is not possible for us to be outside the temple but rather we are the temple and there is no place to go or to be. Then our offerings would not be about appeasing the gods. They would be about acknowledging and honoring the balance of life and death.

All life is special.
All life is unique.
All things are alive.
All things speak.
We can never be outside of anything because we are part of the whole.
We can never be just an observer because we are always the observed as well.

Reflecting back on the West, what have you harvested and gathered in?
What can you give back?
What do you give back?

Great offerings were often made at harvest. They showed a level of gratitude, willingness and appreciation. They required a level of trust as well. Offerings were made even when the harvest was meager or poor.

The people had to trust that the earth, the gods and the ancestors would give back in return. They were dealing with matters of life and death. They dared not offer up unwanted, blemished, devalued things. They gave the finest drink, the healthiest animals and the most precious objects of art and finely crafted weapons.

Life was sacred and profane and so was death.

What is the quality of the things you offer up in exchange?

Labyrinth

There may be times when stepping into the North feels like arriving at the center of a labyrinth or reaching your destination at the end of a long pilgrimage. Arriving can carry a sense of awe and wonder, and a desire to offer something up in gratitude. A profound hush can be felt, and stillness, like the frozen Winter, like the silence of a snowfall.

North is the place of endings and beginnings.

A place you can go to determine what is being asked of you, by life, by circumstance, by the ancestors, by the gods.

North is a place you can go to tell the truth about what you are asking of yourself.

How would this lead you to completion and initiation?

A student mentioned in class that he often associated sacrifice with material things such as pouring high-quality alcohol out onto the ground. He said at times he felt like he was wasting something really good.

I asked if he would feel that way if the offering was a carrot from the garden.

Would you differentiate between dropping a piece of fine jewelry or a beautiful work of art into a well and pouring out mead onto the ground or leaving grain in the field?

Is mead less valuable than a hammered piece of gold jewelry?

Is it easier to offer up a carrot than it is a prized weapon?

Do your answers have to do with the monetary value you place upon something or your attitude around the amount of work that was put into creating an object?

There is no need for moralizing or judging.

Asking questions opens up new ways of seeing.

Your answers may interestingly reflect your attitude toward growing old and dying.

Have you ever thought about death as being the way you give back to the earth, to the ancestors, to the cycle?

If death is a way of giving, is it true then that there is more happiness in giving than there is in receiving?

Is it better to offer yourself up in death than it is to be given life?

Or are they equal exchange?

Teiwaz

The vibration of Teiwaz can be strongly felt in the North. It is commonly associated with truth telling, the god Tyr and the sacrifice he made of his hand. He placed it in the mouth of Fenrir, the wolf that brings death and destruction at Ragnarok. This is the battle that will usher in the end, which will also be the beginning, which may in fact have already occurred.

The story holds many layers of meaning with regard to sacrifice and truth.

What if our sacrifice is based upon a compromise?
What if our sacrifice is based upon a lie?

The tale of Tyr and the wolf is almost always told in a way that favors the god and maligns the wolf. As the story goes, the wolf was taken from his mother when he was still small. As he has grown his strength has increased and the gods are no longer able to control him. Several attempts to bind him have failed. His freedom will ultimately bring an end to the gods. Finally, magical fetters that can constrain him are forged by the dwarves but he must be approached in order to be bound. The gods convene and it is decided that Tyr is the one who must go to the wolf. He must lie about the true strength and purpose of the fetters. He tells Fenrir that they are not strong and will not hold and to convince the wolf, Tyr places his hand as a pledge in the wolf's mouth. As soon as the wolf discovers he has been tricked and the bindings cannot be broken, he bites off the hand of Tyr.

In this telling, the god was willing to offer up a sacrifice for what appears to be the greater good. This is not unlike many other stories of sacrifice where some object of great value, or an animal or a human is offered up in the belief that it serves the greater good.
War is an example of this.

There is another side to this story. One that is rarely told. It is from the perspective of the wolf. Tyr was the one who raised the wolf. They had a connection, a relationship from the past. For the wolf this is a story of lies, trickery, and betrayal.

From this perspective, is it truly a story of sacrifice and if so, how can it be justified?

Are there any places in your life where you have been less than truthful, perhaps resorting to trickery to accomplish something? Have you suffered for it and then justified the suffering by saying it was for the greater good?

And was it?

In times past, maidens were thrown into volcanoes as sacrifices to appease the fire gods.

Bulls were killed and their blood poured out upon the ground in the belief that this was necessary to insure an abundant harvest.

We still sacrifice our young men to war, sending them to fight against a perceived enemy, believing it is justified and necessary to keep peace, maintain freedom and preserve what we believe is rightfully ours.

Millions of people belong to a religion that teaches that it was necessary to sacrifice an innocent man in order for sins to be absolved.

Are these beliefs and actions the same?

Are they different?

Another aspect of Teiwaz is regarding integrity and alignment. It has been called Frigga's Spindle. Frigga is a Norse goddess often portrayed as spinning thread. Her distaff points to the Pole Star, the North Star. The star appears to hold still while the entire Northern sky circles around it. The Pole Star was and still is used to navigate, to locate and way find. You could say that Teiwaz points the way to your true North, your integrity, your honesty, your sovereignty.

Teiwaz could merge with the staff you bring into the Center when you wish to align with your truth.

The North is a good place to explore truth telling and our willingness to say no to others so we can say yes to ourselves. How often do you say yes to others because you want to be nice or because you do not want to appear selfish or uncaring? What happens to you when you say yes to others at your own expense?

Standing in the North and aligning with Teiwaz we can feel the places in our life where we have become out of balance. The truth is when we over-commit, over-give or auto-give, we become tired, resentful, angry, and bitter. And when that happens, we can no longer be trusted. That is a hard truth to hear.

If for instance you are in the field of care giving or service and you do not take care of yourself, you cannot be trusted.
Would you go to a dentist who has bad teeth?
Even though she might be expert in her field, she cannot be trusted to take care of anyone's teeth if she does not take care of her own.

If you spend all your time and energy taking care of others and worrying about their needs and wants but neglect your own, you cannot be trusted.
Standing in the North helps you find your North Star, your true North, so you can live with honor, integrity and truth.
This will bring you back to Center and sovereignty.

Your willingness to ask and answer questions about sacrifice and offerings requires the stillness and silence that can be found in the North.

Discovering the answers will lead you to the place of initiation.

Initiation

Initiation rituals have long been part of the human experience just as sacrifice rituals have been. Initiation means a beginning or an entrance or a going in. It is usually associated with a rite of passage ceremony and it can signify a transformation or rebirth into a new role or a new life. Initiation ceremonies are still practiced today in rituals such as baptism, graduation and marriage, or mystery rites required to gain entrance into a religious order, secret society or fraternal organization.

Some types of initiation involve rites and rituals that are limited to a few, select individuals who are called to a vocation such as shaman, medicine woman or warrior. Coming to the point of an initiation may require lengthy training, sacrifices and pilgrimages or vision quests. Initiations such as these often involve deeply altered states of consciousness that might present as a terrible accident or a life-threatening, potentially fatal illness or a psychological crisis. Such initiations can at times cause death. If not actual death, then the initiate experiences a death-like state which could include things such as feelings of dismemberment, burial or shattering. Some people may engage in initiation rites in order to open up their awareness of and connection with unseen beings, ancestors or gods.

The North holds the energy of coming to a place in life where you know that what you have been doing and how you have been living no longer fits. It no longer satisfies you and you want to live with greater awareness and integrity. You may have reached a point where you are finished with living your life or telling the story of your life from the place of a victim. Initiation must come from the place of willingness to sacrifice, offer up and complete.

Accountable

Step back into the Center.
Claim your sovereignty.
Acknowledge the past and the things that have happened.
Be accountable for your own choices.
Take responsibility for the consequences of those choices.
Stop carrying guilt or allowing others to make you feel guilty and responsible for things that happened in the past before you were born.

Ask yourself the questions,

Who am I?
Where am I?
What time is it?
What do I need?
Which way is the wind blowing?

Stop comparing your pain, suffering, loss or trauma to that of others, believing that somehow your experiences are worse, more intense or extreme.

Comparing does not serve you or anyone for that matter.
What happened to you happened to you and no one else.
Do not perpetuate separation by living as a victim.
Learn ways to speak honestly about the truth of your life and
your experiences and find your way back to your Center.
You long for something different and for that to happen you
must be willing to change, to let go, to give up the identity you
have created for yourself by the stories you tell about your suffering.
Speak instead about how you were affected and how you survived.
Reclaim your sovereignty and power.

Like the acorn you must let go of the tree and drop to the
ground in order to grow into your own unique self. The acorn
can be nothing other than an oak tree but it will not grow into
the same tree from which it fell.
You are not benefited by staying on the ground as an acorn and
telling stories about what it was like living life attached to a
tree. So stop believing the stories you tell yourself and others
about who you think you are and why you are the way you are.
Like the acorn, you were formed by the past but in order to
grow into something new you must let go.
Step into the North.
Forget who you have been.
Offer up who you are now so you can transform into what is
next.

Aging And Death

Have you ever thought about birth as being an initiation?
Have you ever thought about death as being an initiation?
When we are born, we are birthed into death.

An imbalance with the energies of the North shows up in the beliefs and practices surrounding old age, the process of dying and death itself.

In our culture there is an almost obsessive drive to stay forever young by attempting to never show signs of aging or imagine that you have not aged.

You only need look at advertising in magazines, on television and the Internet to see how prevalent this imbalance is.

Acceptance of death does not mean you let yourself go or neglect yourself. The acceptance is about acknowledging where you are in your life.

Who am I?

What time is it?

Have you ever heard someone say they are a certain age, maybe 40, 50, or 60 and then follow that statement with 'but I don't look my age'?

What are we supposed to look like at a certain age?

What is the underlying message of that statement?

We are so disturbed by the thought of aging and looking old we spend enormous amounts of money on anti-aging creams and hair color and plastic surgery.

We even pay thousands of dollars to have our bodies embalmed and then placed in metal coffins.

We still rot and decay.

It is inevitable.

Our bodies always return to the earth no matter how long it takes.

We are offerings that feed the future.

We live life as consumers and in the end we shall be consumed, whether we are willing to offer ourselves up or not.

Imbalance might show up in beliefs and behaviors around illness, aging and the debilitation that goes along with growing old.

How do you feel about allowing yourself to die with dignity perhaps even refusing treatment that others believe might keep you alive just a little bit longer, no matter the pain or the cost?

Imbalance may show up in your attitudes and actions around trying to keep your pets alive with heroic measures.
It might show up in your unwillingness to allow your loved ones to die with dignity.
Where else might imbalance show up?

Life exists because of death.
Death is life.
If you are afraid to die, then you are afraid to live.
Participating in life requires a willingness to participate in death. To align with the North is to step into the place of completion and surrender, to offer yourself up to the wisdom of the cycle and place yourself as the sacrifice, willing to have the experience of initiation into what is next.

What do you believe about death and why?
Do you embrace growing old and dying?
North is a place where you can truly test yourself.

Silence And Stillness

People may use the words silence and stillness as if they are interchangeable.

They are not.

Silence does not mean there is no sound. It is the absence of irrelevant noise. There is silence in the forest even in the presence of birdsong, small creatures rustling in the leaves and the wind in the evergreens.

It is not silent if someone is talking or music is playing or a generator is operating.

There are different kinds of silence.

The silence of the eyes.

The silence of the heart.

These too can be found in the North.

Stillness is associated with a state of bodily rest.

You can be very still in your body even when you are surrounded by noise.

You can be in silence and still have your body be busy or in motion.

Silence will often foster stillness.

Stillness will often foster silence.

When you find yourself in a truly silent environment, you may desire to come into stillness with your physical body.

Stillness in your physical body can support inner stillness.

Do you find it challenging to just sit in silence without music, without interfering sound?

The runes whisper.

You cannot hear what is being whispered when you are constantly bombarded with noise.

Isa And Ice

In the North you can develop and strengthen your relationship with Winter, the dark, the cold, the stillness and ice.
This in turn deepens your relationship with the runes, especially with Isa, the rune of ice. Ice is a crystal. The signature of Isa is a straight, vertical line. It holds all the runes, dismantled line by line and then stacked and layered on top of each other. Its multi-dimensional appearance is much like a glacier with its layers upon layers of frozen history. In my rune poems I speak of Isa as home to all the runes.

A very ancient and powerful force is acting on the ice at this time.
What is happening is part of an endless cycle of freezing and melting, a cycle of fire and ice.
It is the creation story of our Northern European ancestors.
What time is it?
Which way is the wind blowing?

Who are these winds that are blowing right now, causing the weather to change and the ice to melt?
They must be working together with Kari, the North Wind.
He has a special relationship with cold and ice.
There must be some sort of agreement.

The winds are alive.
We inhale them.

They breathe themselves into us.
They are changing the weather, which is melting the ice.
They are providing us with information.
As the ice is melting more rune wisdom is being revealed.

Instead of being afraid of the warming, should we not be
seeking a way to find relationship with these winds of warmth
and ask them to give us understanding from their perspective?
Can they help us understand what is transforming so we can
embrace what is emerging?
As revealed in the West, the stars can only be seen when it is
dark.
What can only be seen or known when the ice melts?

The North reminds us of the creation stories that come from
our European ancestors. These are not stories of life crawling
out of primordial ooze somewhere in the South, in the jungle
or the desert. They are stories of the chaos that occurred in
the beginning that was also the ending, when Muspelheim, the
realm of fire collided with and embraced Niflheim, the realm of
ice. As the ice melted life that was already in form was released.
These stories of emerging in the North hold as much truth as all
the other stories.
Step into the North with a shifted perspective and ask new and
different questions.

As the ice is melting what is being released?

When a volcano erupts under a glacier, steamy explosions of
ash are released into the air while at the same time new land is
being formed.

Great changes are happening right now on the earth and they will continue.
Great and fearsome changes have happened on the earth before, sometimes slowly and sometimes with great speed.
It is a cycle.
The energies that are being released are necessary for whatever is coming into form.

What is happening on the earth is not just about humans.
I am not saying that it is okay for you to throw your garbage in the river or for factories to spew toxins into the air. I am suggesting we consider how manipulated we are and how obsessed we have become because of the one-sided stories we are being told.
The earth is erupting.
She is opening up fissures and chasms.
She is spewing out gases and lava.
She is melting the ice, refilling the aquifers and there is no doubt she is being aided by the winds.
Perhaps she is retching and vomiting, tired of us humans, tired of our greed and stupidity.

Remember the story of the reindeer cow, Audhumbla, emerging from the swirling chaos of fire and ice.
Are we not witnessing creation as well as destruction at this time in earth's history?
Has the great primal cow of the North returned?
Is she in labor?
As she licks the ice, is her hot breath joining forces with the various winds?

Remember, the North teaches us about helplessness and surrender, completion, sacrifice and offering as well as initiation and transformation.

We play a part in this change but the cause of the change is bigger than mere humans and certainly we cannot control it. Something enormous and ancient has been set in motion and it must go through its own cycle.

Do you feel helpless?

Do you feel hopeless?

You can grieve in the North.

You can be sad.

You can participate but perhaps from the place of new and different questions.

You can ask again, where did I enter this never-ending story?

Helpless In The Wind

Have you ever thought about being at the mercy of the wind?

There is a tendency in our modern world to forget our helplessness in the face of the elements and to imagine as well that somehow we can control them or are in control of them.

How helpless are we in the face of the wind when we are unable to start a fire?

How helpless are we when the topsoil of the earth is blowing away as happened during the Dust Bowl years of the American and Canadian prairies?

How helpless are we at sea in a fierce storm?

How many of the great natural disasters are caused by or
involve wind?
Tornados, hurricanes, cyclones, floods. Fire storms.
Wind acting with earth.
Wind acting with water.
Wind·acting with fire.

We trivialize these powerful forces when we think of them as
mere elements.
They are beings, ancient beings.
The most crucial part of understanding any of them is to look
first at their destructive, dangerous, terrifying, unstoppable
nature and remember just how puny and helpless we are in
their presence.
We must never forget.
It is impossible for us as humans to gain mastery over any of
these beings we call elements.

Actual survival was at stake for the ancestors. They had to know
what time it was and which way the wind was blowing. They
needed to know the winds by name.
When a particular wind blew down from the glaciers, they had
to know what kind of weather it was bringing. When Howler,
or Ice Rain or Blizzard Wind blew they prepared for drastic
conditions.
Life depended upon knowing not only which way the wind was
blowing but which wind was blowing.
We may think that our lives no longer depend on such
information.
We may think we do not need to pay attention.

The truth is, we do.
North reminds us we are helpless because we cannot control the wind.

Where in your life do you feel aligned with the teachings of the North?
Where do you feel off-balance?
Are you at a place of initiation?
And if so, into what?
If you leave the North where will you turn next?
Will you face the East?
What wisdom would you bring to the East after having made offerings and sacrifices in the North?

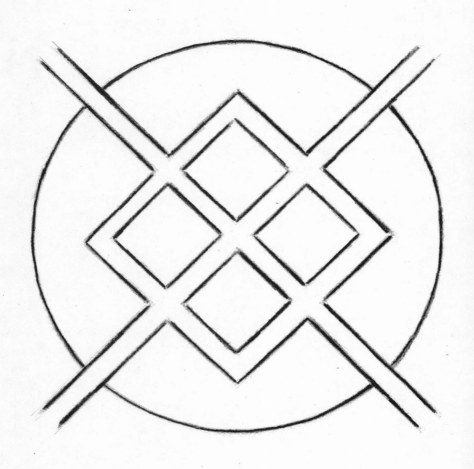

3

USING
THE WHEEL

A TOOL

The Wheel is a tool.
A simple tool.
A complicated tool.
A useful tool with unlimited possibilities.
The more you use it the more you will come to appreciate its value.
It is powerful, adaptable and individual.
The Wheel provides a framework for a daily practice that is simple yet complex.
You do not need some special formula or set of rules.
All you need is a willingness to stand courageously in the Center of your own life, in alignment with integrity, honor and accountability and claim your sovereignty.
Ask the questions.
They will always bring you back into your body and into the present moment.
In any situation, any location, any circumstance.

Who am I?
Where am I?
What time is it?
What do I need?
Which way is the wind blowing?

The answers may not come quickly.
Do not try to rush them.
Do not over-think.
Be silent.

Be still.
Listen.
Connect with the Tree.
Feel the answers rise up from the roots into your body.
Answer with your heart not your mind.

We can use the Wheel as a map to access rune wisdom.
We may try to imagine how our ancestors would have used the
Wheel but the truth is, we do not know if they even had such a
tool.
What we do know is that they oriented themselves upon the
earth using the horizon.

I intentionally did not draw any runes on the Wheel fearing that
the reader would be led to believe that they belonged only in
the places where they were drawn. The runes are constantly
moving in and out of all the directions, circling around the
Wheel as the Wheel is turning.

There is no specific color attached to any one direction.
There are no animals or birds that represent one place.
You do not need to turn in a certain way to do it right.
Fire does not belong in the South nor water in the West.
It is not necessary to wear special clothing, avoid certain foods
or alcohol, stand on one leg or howl at the moon.

Whenever you come in contact with such rigid rules and
formulas always remember that at some point in time, someone
made them up.
So make up your own rituals.
Do things in a way that feels right for you.

Turn in the direction you want.

Listen for which rune is calling to you.

Over time you may find that your actions connect you with your ancestors, tapping into their memories and wisdom and this may add insight and meaning to the way you are doing things.

What I offer here are only suggestions.

They may or may not work for you.

There is no right way to use the Wheel.

There is no wrong way.

Be willing to take your time.

Be patient, open and vulnerable.

Practice.

Explore.

Listen.

Use a staff.

It will prove to be a powerful ally.

Use the runes.

Begin in the Center.

That is where you always are.

Take a breath.

Ask yourself the questions,

Who am I?

Where am I?

What time is it?

What do I need?

Which way is the wind blowing?

Come home to yourself.
Remember who you are.
Be courageous.
Stand with honor and integrity, in alignment and balance.
Claim sovereignty in the Center of your own life.

A woman in one of my classes, after pondering the questions, stepped into the Center and declared,

I am an artist.
I am in my center.
I am safe in my home.
It is time for me to stop giving myself away.
I need to take care of myself first.
I need to feed my artist.

Another individual stepped into the Center and spoke,

I am a wise man.
I am right here, right now.
It is not the past.
It is not the future.
I can see forward.
I can see backward.
What time is it?
Well, the sun just went down.
I need to be alone tonight.
I need a vacation from screen time.
The wind is blowing in from the Midwest and it is carrying with it
the smell of some old, family drama.

A third person said with some hesitation,

*I am a woman standing in the middle of a life that no longer
suits me.*
It is time for me to tell the truth to myself and to others.
I need to believe in myself and have the courage to take action.
*The winds of change are blowing and I'm going to let them carry
me away.*

You can see from these examples that the questions can be
answered in many different ways and the answers you give may
be different each time. They can be literal, general, figurative,
explicit, even precise.
It does not matter.
There are no right answers.
There are no wrong answers.
What is important is that you are standing in the Center.

Bring The Runes Into The Circle

Standing in the Center you will feel the presence of the Tree.
You may embrace it, encircle it, touch it or even merge with
it. The trunk connects the roots below the surface with the
branches above. Energy moves down and up, yet the Tree
remains in the same place. You see from above what you know
from below.
The roots draw from the Wells. The branches talk with the Winds.
This is your body and your mind in harmony with the earth.

Once you are firmly planted in the Center connected with the
Tree, you can bring in the runes.

You may decide to do this in a certain order or sequence or you may choose to draw them out of the pouch one by one. You will want to explore each one of them individually in relationship to the Center and then move out into all of the directions.

Bringing runes into the Circle gives us opportunity to become aware of the landscape of our personal life. What we need depends upon time and circumstance.

There are no rules that say that a specific rune belongs in a certain direction.

Each rune is a unique being who embodies multiple energies. They unfold and reveal at their own pace. Some may feel more familiar to you than others. That is normal. They are individuals.

Remember, there is no right way to do it.
There is no should or supposed to.
You may wish to work with a new rune each day.
Or you may linger with the same one for a week or longer.
Do not rush this process.
Do not try to hurry through it as if it were some kind of race or contest.
Do not question how long it takes you, imagining that somehow you should be able to do it faster.

Reach In The Pouch

Standing in the Center, reach in the pouch and draw out a rune. Hold it in your hand. Whisper its name. Feel its vibration. Perhaps you selected Ansuz, a rune related to language, a rune about creating with words, speaking things into existence. Because it is about speaking and language it is also about air, the movement of air that naturally occurs when we speak.

The movement of air changes the weather.
Remembering that the Center is about alignment and integrity
you might ask,

Are the words I speak in alignment with truth?
Are they rooted in wisdom?
Do I say what I mean?
What kind of climate do I create with my language?
Am I speaking from the place of the victim?
Do I use my voice to intimidate or to empower?

These might be questions for one day.
The next time Ansuz appears you might explore how your
words can be used to speak out against injustice. Or how they
could be the leafy branches of a tree that provide shade, a
place where others can find protection and peace.

Select another rune. Hold it. Feel it. Listen to it.
Perhaps you have chosen Ior, a rune associated with the World
Serpent, Jormungund. Its thrashing in the great oceans causes
destruction and chaos on the earth. Life could not continue if
the oceans were always calm.
Life and death exist in the same motion.
Another teaching of this rune is about boundaries and borders.
How can you be on both sides of something at the same time?
Ior shows that chaos and destruction must exist at all times in
perfect balance and harmony with the continuation of life.

You might wonder what connection the World Serpent has with
the Tree. The Tree holds the answer. There are parts of it that are

hidden and parts of it that are seen. They are both necessary for the whole to function and one is not more valuable than the other nor do they exist separately.

Ior's message is, pay as much attention to what is not seen as you do to what is seen. It takes courage to live this way.

Once you have worked with each rune individually in the Center you will feel ready to bring them individually into each of the four directions.

What relationship exists between Ansuz and the East, the place of emerging, anticipation and birth?

What words emerge from your mouth?

What do you give birth to when you speak?

Are you a good listener or do you always try to anticipate what is going to be said next?

What wisdom would Dagaz bring into the West?

West is the direction of Equinox.

How does equal night and equal day, equal dark and equal light, resonate with what is currently happening in your life?

What is transforming over and over again?

Are you in the middle, at the still point, willing to be both and neither?

What happens when Dagaz is brought into the North or the South?

Both of these directions hold extremes, the longest night of Winter Solstice and the longest day of Summer Solstice.

Where in your life do you find extremes?

Are they necessary or are they causing imbalance?

You will find that some runes fit easily into one direction and yet seem to have little or no connection with another. That is natural. Remember they are beings with personalities and characteristics. If this happens, bring in more runes and see what they have to say collectively.

Standing in the Center you might draw Sowelo from the pouch and decide to turn and face the East, the place where the sun rises up. It may speak to you of Spring and how the sun melts the snow, providing the warmth and light that is needed for plants to sprout and grow. Sowelo might ask to be carried into the South where it reminds you that the sun can also scorch and burn, blind and kill. It holds both life and death just as Berkana does. Sowelo in the North might provide the hope necessary to survive the Winter.
All runes embody the balance of opposites.

What is the weather like in the garden of your life?
Does it rain a lot?
Then Sowelo wisdom could be very helpful.
Is the climate hot and arid?
Laguz may be needed.
You may wish to connect with Othila to define the space of your home and garden and use the wisdom of both Sowelo and Laguz to create balance between water and the sun.
Jera holds a truth present in nature. The harvest cannot be rushed nor can it be delayed. Jera maintains the harmony that must exist between the turning of the Wheel of the seasons in nature and your own cycles and rhythms.
Ingwaz, a rune so evident in the fertility of Spring and so comfortable in the East works in the South as well.

Life is filled with creativity. Creatures must be both virile and fecund. Plants must mature and go to seed so they can reproduce. The presence of Fehu roots us in the earth, reminding us that all wealth comes from the land.

In another instance you may want clarification or understanding in one specific direction. For example, you are called to the North desiring guidance and wisdom regarding what you are being asked to offer up and what initiation and transformation might occur from such an offering.
You reach in the pouch and select three runes, one for the direction of the North, one for the sacrifice and one for the transformation.

The Wheel is divided into dark and light and gradations of each, just like the actual year. You may need to live in a more balanced way by embracing and appreciating them both. You reach in the pouch and select a rune for the dark and a rune for the light. Listen to both of them and what they have to say about the side they are on and then ask them what they want to share with you about the other side.
Or you could select three runes from the pouch, one each for the past, present and future. Taking up the runes you ask,

What does the rune representing the past tell me about the dark?
What does it say about the light?
What does the rune of the present know about the dark and about the light?
What does the rune of the future tell me about both sides?

Toss The Runes

In order to toss the runes you will need a casting cloth that is illustrated with the Wheel or perhaps you can draw the Wheel yourself on a large piece of paper or enlarge and copy the drawing from page 26 in this book.

You can take a handful of runes from the pouch and toss them onto the Wheel and see who shows up and in which direction.

Which runes are present in the East, the place of anticipation and emerging?

Did a rune land in the Center aligning with sovereignty?

What does it have to say about integrity?

What wisdom about harvest and discernment is being shared by the runes that landed in the West?

How can this wisdom be used in making decisions?

Who is in the South and what do they say about allowing things to unfold and evolve at their own pace?

What runes have placed themselves in the light half of the year and who is in the dark half?

Find Your Way Back

The world is constantly changing.

We are constantly changing.

And even though each person's life and circumstances are unique and individual we all need the same things to live. We must be connected to the earth, in rhythm with the seasons. We must orient ourselves with the setting and the rising of the sun.

The teachings of the Wheel and the wisdom of the runes are gifts to us from our ancestors. They are fluid and alive. They provide us with direction and guidance. They do not tell us how we should or should not do something but rather they teach us to listen, ask questions and remind us to trust our own inner wisdom. Life on earth thrives because of diversity. Our answers to the questions vary depending upon where we are, who we are, what time it is and the direction the wind is blowing.
And the darkness continues to rise up and the sun continues to set.

There are many ways to use the runes together with the Wheel. And you can use the Wheel without the runes.
For instance, there might be a time when you feel ungrounded, overwhelmed, off balance. Stress may be causing you to disconnect from your body or the present moment. You may be in need of some clarification or direction.
Stop.
Take a breath.
Step back into your Center and connect with the Tree.
You have roots and branches.
Let the roots stabilize and ground you.
Climb up into the branches to gain an overview or a different perspective. Remember that the squirrel running up and down the trunk can restore the connection between your body and your mind.
Be still, knowing that the Tree is not going anyplace and yet, there is movement in the stillness.
You are back in the Center, in the present moment.
Reclaim your sovereignty and align with your integrity.

From this position you can ask and answer the questions,

Who am I?
Where am I?
What time is it?
What do I need?
Which way is the wind blowing?

Take your time. Ponder each question. Allow the answers to rise
up out of the roots and move through the trunk. Once you feel
complete with this you can choose which direction you would
like to face.

Does it feel like something new is emerging in your life?
Would you turn to the East or perhaps another direction?
Are you unsure of what it is or do you know?
Do you need help in determining how to care for it?
Is it arising from the soil or did it float in on a current of air?
Is it now taking root?
What could you come to understand by turning and stepping
into the South?
What might the West or the North have to say?

The questions open up so many other options.
Pay attention.
Sense what you are feeling.
What is happening?
Are you moralizing?
Do you judge yourself or discount your own answers, perhaps
even trying to modify them or ignore them?

Most of us are very comfortable with trying to think of the right answer.

It can be quite a surprise for us when our body speaks, when we hear answers rising up spontaneously from our heart, our gut or our intuition.

We may feel a bit startled or even fearful of our responses as they rise up from below the surface, from the roots.

We may try to convince ourselves that these answers cannot possibly be right or that what we are feeling is not okay. It is bad or selfish or even unhealthy.

So we go looking for another answer, a different answer.

Our mind is often trying to protect us from some old experience or from something that happened in the past and has nothing to do with the present moment.

If this is happening you may find it helpful to return to the Center and go through the questions again,

Who am I?
Where am I?
What time is it?
What do I need?
Which way is the wind blowing?

Creatures Appear

It is not unusual for animals or birds to appear when you work with the runes and meditate with the Wheel. When this happens take the time to connect with them. Avoid trying to attach a preconceived meaning to their visit. It might be the squirrel Ratatoskr or the dragon serpent Nidhogg. It might be the Fenris wolf or a reindeer, perhaps even Audhumbla. Horses often gallop in with Ehwaz or Raido, or the aurochs with Uruz, a wolf with Skadi and Yr, a bear with Nauthiz.

I often feel the presence of ravens in the West. Perhaps the reason I do is because I experience West as a place of death and disappearing. Ravens connect me to dark wisdom. Sometimes I ponder the saga of Odin's ravens, Hugin and Munin, who are said to represent thought and memory. They flew away each day and then returned with the dark as the sun was setting.

Just because the ravens visit me in the West does not mean that they will come to you or even that they should come to you. You might have a different relationship with these black birds. The important thing to remember is you do not always need to go to a book to look up a meaning written by someone else.
If a raven appears, in any of the directions, ask,

What do I know about ravens?

Then wait.
See what information comes to you.
Feel what you remember.
Trust your own knowing.
You might say ravens are black.
That is what I know and black is about the dark.
Ravens are carrion birds.
They are often found in places of death such as battlefields or cemeteries.

You might ask,

Is the bird flying away from me or toward me?
Is the bird flying away from a battlefield or flying toward one?
Is it on my shoulder?
Is it bringing me information?
Am I the raven?

Try asking the raven why it appeared.

Another animal I personally connect with in the West, in the autumn, is the wild boar. Boars are very active in the fall. They root around for acorns and mushrooms. They serve a valuable purpose in the forest. Their digging and rooting help to aerate the soil by disturbing it. They spread seeds and spores. Boars are fierce and protective. They can eat almost anything. I wonder about the boar and ask it what it came to share with me. And I wonder what it would have to say to me if I encountered it in the East.

The more you use the Wheel the more valuable and familiar it will become.
Each time you step into the Center you will be presented with new challenges and opportunities.

RUNES FOR AN UPCOMING YEAR

Using the Wheel to do a rune casting or rune placement for an upcoming year can provide you with a meaningful map full of patterns, progressions, insights and wisdom. It does not and will not predict the future. It provides you with a glimpse of the energies that are present and coming into form.

You might wish to cast the Wheel at the beginning of a new year. It could be based on the calendar year or the seasonal year. You might want to cast the Wheel to mark your birthday and the coming year ahead. It could be for an anniversary or the beginning of something new such as a relationship or career, a move or the start of a project, adventure, commitment or personal journey.

I have used the Wheel as a tool for myself as well as for many who come to me seeking rune wisdom and guidance.

Once you decide to cast the Wheel you will need to set aside sufficient, uninterrupted time to experience and complete the process. I find it helpful to dedicate several hours or even a large part of a day so I can set my intention as well as have time to meditate on the runes chosen and journal about any thoughts and feelings that arise.

You may want to make it part of a ritual, lighting candles, burning incense, making an offering.
You may want to do it at a special time such as a fully enshadowed moon or a fully reflecting moon, or at an equinox or solstice.

And all this being said, you will gain great value from the experience even if you have only an hour and all you can do is the casting.

Patterns and repeats appear.

Cycles and rhythms are evident.

Awareness is heightened.

Insight is gained.

It is a meaningful experience.

Creating A Rune Wheel

Use a set of 33 runes.

Always draw from a full pouch.

Begin in the Center. It is the present moment.

Feel yourself standing in your sovereignty, in the Center of your own life.

Who are you in this present moment as you begin this new cycle?

Who do you desire to be through the coming year?

How can you stand with courage, honor and integrity, aligning yourself with truth?

Reach in the pouch and draw a rune.

If you feel called to select more than one rune for the Center, do that.

It is your choice.

You may have the experience of runes sticking together, as if they do not want to come out alone.

Honor that.

It might also happen that a rune or runes simply jump out of the pouch or drop onto the floor.

Remember, they are alive and individual and have their own personalities and agendas.

Mark the rune or runes in the Center of the Wheel.

Return them to the pouch and mix them up.

Once you have done this for the Center, decide which season or direction feels right and turn your attention there.

For example, you might be doing this casting for your birthday, which happens to be around the time of the Winter Solstice.

Looking at the Wheel, the quarter section that holds Winter Solstice is North and it contains the words Sacrifice and Transform.

Reach in the pouch and select a rune for the solstice keeping in mind that Winter Solstice is the longest night of the year.

Mark the rune on the Wheel. Put it back in the pouch and mix them all up.

Next draw a rune for the word Sacrifice. Mark it down, return it to the pouch and mix them all up.

Draw a rune for the word Transform and do the same thing.

Remember there might be times when more than one rune wants to come out of the pouch. Trust that that is what needs to happen.

Continue on around the Wheel, season by season, direction by direction, drawing runes for the solstices and the equinoxes as well as the words in each quadrant.

Remember to draw from a full pouch.

When you have finished you will have marked 13 runes on the Wheel, possibly more if there were multiples that came out together.

Take your time and look at the runes.

Do you see any repeats?

Sometimes the same rune will appear many times in a year.

Do you see any repeats in a sequence?

What about shapes?

How many runes have center still points such as Gebo, Gar, Mannaz and Dagaz?

How many runes from the Jotnar Aett are present?

They carry energies that are quite different from those of the Elder Futhark.

It is meaningful to take note of what runes are not present.

You might want to note the runes that appear in a direction or season that holds energies that are seemingly opposite.

For instance, do fire runes appear in the Winter or death runes in the Spring?

Is there a strong presence of movement runes such as Raido and Ehwaz or turning, spinning runes such as Jera and Eihwaz?

Do not be quick to read the runes, attaching meanings to them.

Consider each rune individually and get a sense of how it feels to you.

Do this before you look up anything in a book.

If you are using a journal or notebook, write about them.

What do you see?

Does the shape hold any special meaning for you?

Where are some places you have seen it before?

How does the rune sound?

What emotions does it stir up?

Is there any particular place in your body where you feel it more intensely than other places?

What runes are on either side of it?

What runes are opposite it on the Wheel?
After taking time to do this you may want to go to the book and read the poem associated with the rune as well as the brief description.

Remember you have just done a rune casting for an entire year, a complete cycle, the turning of the Wheel.
It contains a lot of information.
The runes are not foretelling the future but rather calling your attention to energies and vibrations that are already present. You get to choose how you are going to interact and participate. The warp threads of the great tapestry of life have already been set on the loom by the Nornir. You get to decide how you weave your own weft threads into the pattern of the Wyrd that is already woven.

Keep a record of the casting in a place that is easily visited. As the Wheel of the year turns, follow it on the calendar, perhaps using the phases of the moon as markers in addition to the seasons. Each time you come to a rune you have marked on the Wheel, do a new reading, perhaps asking what additional wisdom is available for this particular rune at this particular time.

Schedule and plan for these readings so you do not forget. As you use the Wheel of Life together with the runes you will be amazed at how it roots you in the present moment providing you with perspective and depth, at the same time allowing you to see what is beyond the horizon.

4

THE
RUNE BEINGS

32 PLUS ONE

The runes are commonly divided into groups called aetts, a word that is equivalent to clan or a social group with a common descent. Each group holds eight runes.

Fehu Aett

Hagalaz Aett

Teiwaz Aett

Most people are familiar with the 24 runes found in these three groupings. They are referred to as the Elder Futhark. In fact, there are some rune workers who will only use these 24.

When the ancestors gave me the vision of the lost teachings I was shown the rune Gar as a center point around which 32 runes were circling, not just 24. I believe that these additional eight runes are the runes of the primal giants and so I group them together into a fourth aett I call the Jotnar Aett. There are other rune workers who group them in the same way.

When Odin tore a hole in the Web, runes poured forth. It is possible that these additional runes were part of the ones received at that time by the giant Alsvith. This is spoken of in the Hávamál stanza 144.

There are various spellings for each of the runes as well as various pronunciations. Some of them are shown with slightly different shapes such as Hagalaz with two diagonal lines, or Jera formed by Isa with two Kenaz shapes attached, one on each side of the vertical line. There is also a version of Yr that is drawn without a horizontal line, the short vertical line floating in the middle. Calc is another one. It sometimes appears as an inverted Algiz.

As I have come to know the runes through listening to them, I have found that the various shapes carry slightly different energies, rather like the black half-note keys on a piano.

The 33 rune poems written in this book are my original creations. Each poem is composed using only 33 words. They first appeared in print in the limited edition, handmade, leather-bound book called (un) familiar. The story of its creation can be found on my website.

The drawings featured in this book are the work of artist Naomi St. Clare. The style she used to draw the runes is based upon her own feelings and experiences with them.

Anyone interested in the runes discovers quite quickly that there are shelves of rune books, each author offering their own version of what a rune means or how to interpret it or how to use it. Do not become fixated on trying to find the one right book or the one right meaning. There is value in all of them. You may find it useful to gather many books together and compare their explanations. As your relationship with the runes develops you will begin to hear them speaking to you personally and you will be shown many variations and connections.

As I have stated elsewhere in this book, the runes are alive and they vibrate with wisdom. They form and inform each other and present various aspects of themselves depending on which ones appear together in a casting or a reading.
I share here some very basic rune meanings based upon my personal experiences with them. I encourage you to read my

book *The Runes Revealed—an (un) familiar journey* to gain further insight and understanding from my perspective.

As the ice is melting, more and more runes are being revealed. They hold the sounds of destruction and creation. We have only just begun to truly grasp the magnitude of the runes. They are without number just like the stars.

Coming to know the runes, developing relationships with them, even remembering their shapes and names can be a daunting task. You are learning a new language with all its complexities and subtleties, within the context of time and location. Be patient. Be willing to listen. Learning to use and live with the wisdom of the runes and the Wheel takes time. You will be rewarded.

I often suggest to those who are new to the runes, and even to those who are not, to create a system using index cards or something similar. Mark a rune shape and its name on each card. If the rune has variations in its shape or spelling, you might want to include them as well. Use the back of the card to make notes about the meanings, the feelings, the experiences you have with each rune as it appears to you, as you read about it, as you meditate with it or even hear it.
Do not be tempted to rely upon one source for definition and meaning.
There is no one true interpretation.
There is no one right meaning.
Start a collection of books about the runes. Each author will share a new perspective based on their personal experience and understanding.

Trust yourself and your own relationship with these ancient beings.
Let the ancestors guide you.
Listen to the runes as they vibrate.
Feel them in your body.

Do they harmonize?
Do they align?
Do they restore balance?
What value do they bring into your life?

You will quickly discern the places where you are out of tune.
Your experiences and insights are just as valid, just as true as anyone else's.
The ancestors, the gods and the Jotunfolk are still with us.
Why would we think that they only had dealings with humans in the past?
Bring each rune, one by one, into each direction.

I have named the runes as I know them.
The artist has drawn them as she sees them.
The explanations are mere snippets of information.
Use the information as a starting place.
Remember, they are multi-faceted, complex individuals and we can never know all there is to know.

My personal experiences over the years have shown me that I have more connection and intimacy with some of the runes than I do others. Some I am drawn to. Some feel really foreign to me. And I am constantly being amazed by their wisdom.
You may also have such experiences.

Allow them to come to you. Do not try to force them into a mold of your or anyone else's making.

I like to illustrate it this way. You may have met me at a book signing event and know me as an author and educator. You may have seen me in a yarn shop buying yarn for my next knitting project. You do not know that I milked cows in my grandmother's barn on a small ranch in northern California and you might be shocked to see me pass you in the fast lane on the freeway, dressed in black leathers and riding my Harley. I would wave.

Let the runes surprise you.
May your journey with them
lead you home.

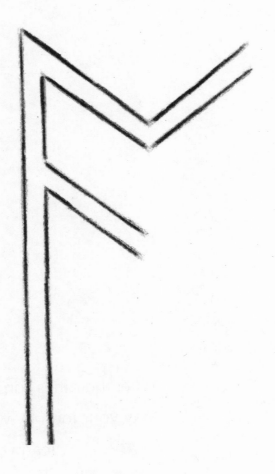

A⟨

mighty Ac
lightning struck
guardian
oak of the myrkwood
nothing is as it seems
Angrboda loved trickery
impregnated
she burst open with monstrosities
birthed destruction
mothered death
who has eaten
her burned heart

Ac is the mighty oak tree, strong and ancient, a sacred guardian,
a doorway into the realm of Other, into the Myrkwood inhabited
by Jotunfolk who shape shift and border cross. Angrboda loves
this rune. This fearsome she-wolf gave birth to children that
bring fear into the hearts of the gods. Oaks are often struck by
lightning. They split open. Oak wood is used for thresholds,
doors and ships, different ways of passing from one place
to another. Ac can invite you to enter into places that might
frighten you. She might ask you to consider what it means
to give birth to something no one loves or to be someone or
believe something that is not acceptable. Do you guard places
where things change form, are not what they seem to be? There
is an element of patience present in this rune. The oak takes
many years to mature and many years to produce a crop of
acorns. Are you willing to wait?

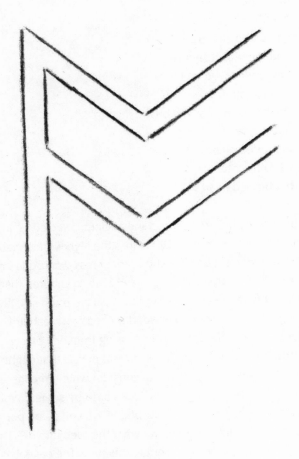

you breathe me
Os
the in and out
of all things
will you share
the poetic mead
fermented
from god spittle and blood
once
the word is spoken
it can never be returned

Os. The in and out of all things. The first breath at birth. The last breath at death. All the breaths in between. The rhythmic in and out of the tides and the chaos that occurs in the estuary when the river is trying to enter the ocean and the tides are pushing it back. Where does the chaos exist in the rhythm? When is there flow and when is there resistance? When the beings of air breathe into us, we are inspired. When they are finished with us, do we expire? Os can be closely linked to Ansuz as well as Laguz. Water and air. What is moving out in your life? What is moving in? When they meet, is there turbulence?

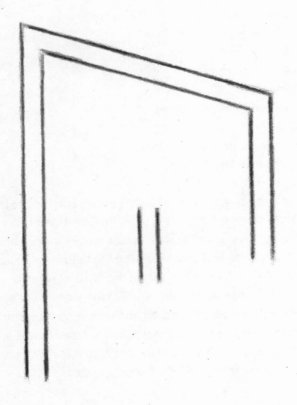

YR

Yr
remind me
to hold focus
with silent aim
your taut bow
Skadi
releases a true flying arrow
you sustain life by taking life
the taste and smell
of blood
are your sacraments

Yr is a favorite of Skadi, the giantess who hunts and skis in the
mountains. She is a wayfinder who reminds us that we must
kill to live. Yr is often associated with a bow and arrow, a tool,
something created that has an intended purpose. You must use
your energy to pull back the arrow before it can fly forward and
hit the target. Skill is demanded as well as aim and focus and
a willingness to release when it is time. There are some who
say that Yr connects with a saddle, something created for a
specific purpose that involves movement and alignment. What
must you do in order to sustain life? Is there a difference for
you when you use a tool that you made yourself and when you
use one made by someone else? What do you need to kill in
your life? Nothing is wasted. When we kill something that no
longer serves us the energy that is released is available to feed
something else.

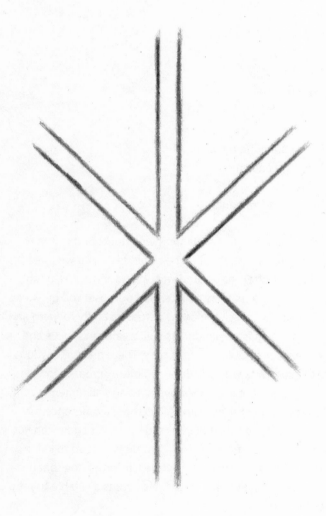

IOR

Ior
I taste you
in the salt
of my body
writhing
the gods cast you away
to avoid the inevitable
you endlessly
devour yourself
standing on the threshold
I partake of you both

Ior and Jormungund, the World Serpent, are wound together. Their thrashing and writhing in the oceans of Midgard cause upheaval and destruction. Tsunamis, hurricanes, erosion and flooding. All of this is necessary and vital for life to continue on earth. There is not always a need to make a choice between one thing and another. Borders enclose and exclude. The sinuous, serpentine body of Jormungund shows us how to be on both sides of a boundary at the same time. Where do you struggle in life feeling you need to make a choice? Are you the straight line that divides or are you the snake with parts of itself on each side? Ior is both. Ior is the Ouroboros, tail in mouth, consuming itself as it sustains.

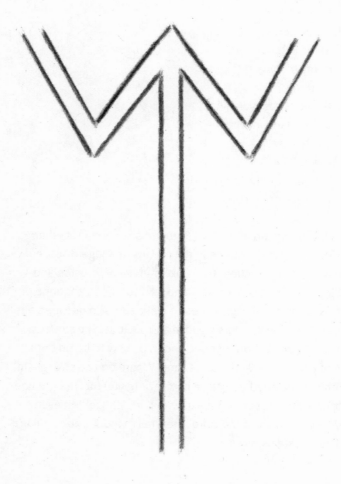

EAR

hanging
on your barbed arms
Ear
I smell death
the rotting stench
there is no choice
in dire necessity
Hela welcomes all
I am inconsequential
reduced to deeds
my body feeds the earth

Ear is the earth grave, the place to which we all return. Some
things take a long time to break down and decompose. This
is the unavoidable end. Our bodies feed the earth. How
comfortable are you with death? What in your life needs to be
buried? Did you lay the dead body out on the kitchen table
and then forget to put it in the grave? Are you sitting around
the table trying to eat dinner pretending the body is not
there? Ear can be seen as the singletree upon which animal
carcasses are hung to be drained and skinned. It is the World
Pillar, the Irminsul, sacred to the Saxons. I wonder at times if its
shape mimics the Amanita mushroom, valued and honored by
our Northern European ancestors and if so, how that weaves
together with death and burial.

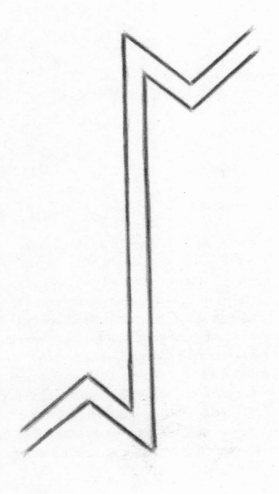

CWEORTH

Cweorth
it is you
fire of Surt
eldest ancestor
who consumes the gods
in the end
your concern is
what must be
at Ragnarok
burn my flesh away
from bone
leaving only ash

Rapid transformation. The funeral pyre is burning with the fires of Cweorth. All fires are the kin of Surt, ancient ancestor present at the beginning when Muspelheim collided with Niflheim. Fire will be there at the end, consuming even the gods. Cweorth activates the release of energy that is held in form. The heat of a wood fire is the warmth of the sun stored in the tree. Cweorth dances together with Eihwaz, energies coming down and energies moving up, life and death. Cweorth asks us to examine what needs to be put to the fire. The very mass that would have extinguished a tiny flame becomes the fuel that feeds the fire once it grows in size. Things placed in the path of molten lava are consumed and transformed.

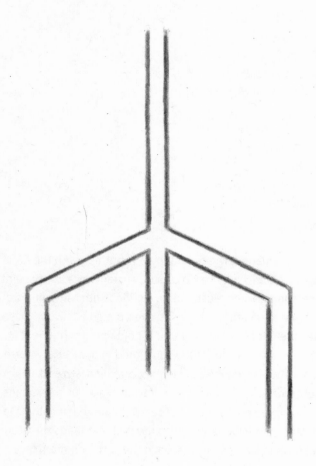

ᚲALᚲ

Calc
I hail thee
raising the mead cup
the gilded horn
I pour out my offerings
to the gods
honoring memory
chalk turns to bone
earth to blood
you provide
nourishment
for Yggdrasil

Calc is the offering cup poured out. What are you willing to offer up so it can be used again? What does your cup contain? Chalk is formed from the skeletal remains of ancient sea creatures compressed by time. It can be used to fertilize the earth. Our offerings feed the soil that feeds us. This is the cycle. The shape of Calc can be seen as the three roots of the World Tree anchoring and stabilizing so new growth can emerge from the center. What can you pour out that feeds your roots so you can grow something new from the midst of the old? The willingness to offer up is a necessary part of transformation.

STAN

Stan
you are the bones of Ymir
killed by kin
you guard
entombed eagles
buried in rock cairns
petrified by salted wind
I stand
by megaliths
unmovable
I wait for them
to open

Stan is ancestor to the giant stone beings who guard the
mouths of burial mounds. Boulders can be obstacles that
present barriers or opportunities. Stan is a megalith holding
memories of the beginning foundations. The very rocks of the
earth were formed from the body of Ymir who was birthed
from the body of Audhumbla, the reindeer mother of us all. The
small offspring of Stan are the stones upon which the runes
are marked, held in the pouch of Pertho. Toss the stones and
take a chance. Lean against the boulders who slowly moved
themselves to form circles of mystery. They will open to those
who are patient enough to wait.

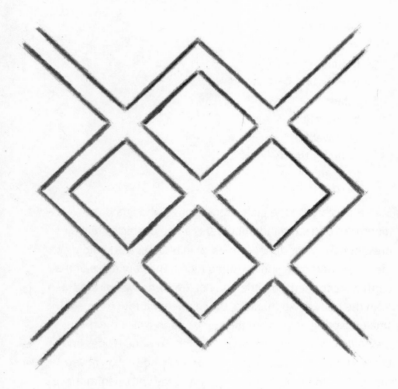

ᚸAR

Gar
gift of Ing
you are the one
who brought them forth
tore a hole
in Ginnungagap
runes
rushed in and out
with piercing wail
the high one
sacrificed himself
ending the beginning

Gar is the gift of Gebo laid over the fertility of Ingwaz, the still point of all that goes forth from the Center. Gar is spear, the spear as a kenning for the World Tree. Gar is distaff, the spindle upon which the universe turns. Its crossed arms extend out in all directions. It creates the pattern of four small Ingwaz runes held in the large Ingwaz. These small circuits within the large form patterns that were walked by the ancestors to activate fertility in the realm of all possibility. Where did you enter the story? At the piercing? When you heard the wail? Through the hole torn in the Web? What is rushing in and what is rushing out? What is circling around your Center?

FEHU

it is you Fehu
the spark
manifested
at the beginning
all wealth
arising from the land
Ymir suckling
Audhumbla licking ice
fearing mortality
I hoard
hinder
withhold
possessed
by possessions
I am consumed

Fehu is energy that has come into form. All wealth comes
from the land. Fehu is most commonly associated with wealth
that is moveable, not stationary. Its assumed connection with
cattle is more likely to be a connection with reindeer. These
migrating herds represented wealth and survival for the
Northern ancestors. You perhaps are being asked by Fehu to
take stock of your belongings and possessions to determine
where they might be slowing you down or feeding off of your
energy creating an imbalance. We must be in constant motion
to remain in balance with Fehu, taking as well as giving back.

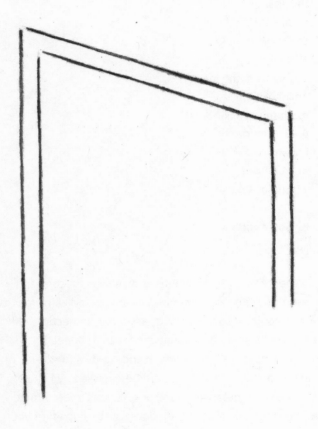

URUZ

I drink to you
mighty aurochs
fearless
formidable
Uruz
it takes courage
to honor a foe
I search for you
in the animal
of my own body
tamed and civilized
I face extinction

Aurochs. This mighty bovine once roamed across Europe
and the British Isles, just as the reindeer did. Uruz speaks to
extinction caused by civilization. What has happened to your
wild, untamed, undomesticated self? We have much to lose
when we attempt to follow all the rules. We honor ourselves
when we accept our wild self. It takes courage to face it. It takes
courage to be it. A good question to explore is, have I tamed
myself into extinction? When we make too many laws, we all
become criminals.

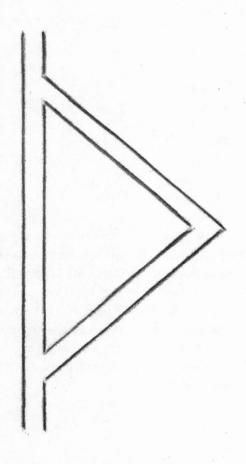

THURISAZ

Ifing the river is called
I will cross over
the bridge
impregnated
by your hammer
expectant
in the storm
you torment and fester
until chaos
births fertility
Thurisaz
my firstborn
belongs to you

Thurs, the Old Norse giants of chaos, were present at the beginning. Their energies are fertile and stormy. They are the chaos that balances order. Great disruption is caused when explosive volcanos erupt under glaciers yet new land is created. Fire melts ice. Thurisaz invites us to explore our relationship with Thor. It is true he is the son of Odin but he is also the son of the giantess, Jord, who is the earth, and the grandson of a giantess as well. In addition, his father Odin carries much giant blood himself. Such ancestry can cause thorny problems for those who desire to be considered descendants of the gods. Which side of the river is more comfortable for you? Thorns can cause us to bleed but do not kill. We might be inclined to use Thurisaz as an enclosure of defense. Remember though, a barrier that is designed to keep things out will at the same time imprison that which is inside.

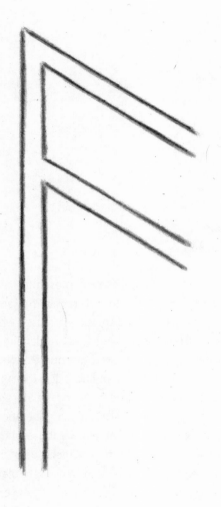

ANSUZ

through you
Ansuz
through the spellsong
a sacrifice screaming
I was spoken into existence
runes poured forth
woven
unbroken
ancestral lines
twisted
by breath and wind
I am the container
I am contained

Ansuz speaks things into existence. We can also do the same. The words we speak become beings. Once they are loose they cannot be returned. Do you use language to create? Do you use language to destroy? Ansuz will hold you accountable for what you say and how you use your voice. Ansuz embodies the wisdom of air. Do we breathe or are we being breathed? Air can reside inside our bodies but not indefinitely. Yet we must reside within the being of air in order to live, just as fish dwell within the being of water. Both Ansuz and Os can connect us with the winds who are air in motion. Moving air changes the weather. What is the climate in your life that surrounds your use of words?

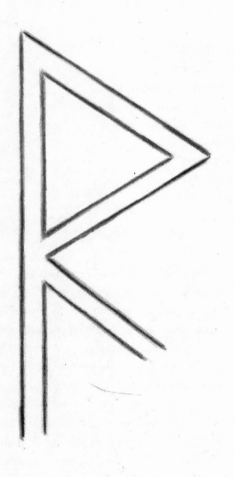

RAIDO

Raido
the adventurer
is on the move
drum and hoof
Odin mounted
moving between worlds
all things change
remain the same
I ride my future
into the past
someone
comes to meet me

There is a rhythmic movement to Raido, the beat of a drum, the gallop of a horse, repetitive movement that allows you to travel between the realms in an altered state. This can be actual travel as well as spiritual journeys. Do you move forward into the future which exists beyond the horizon out of sight? Do you travel back into the past to meet the ancestors? Can you travel to meet yourself without moving? Where are you traveling in your life?

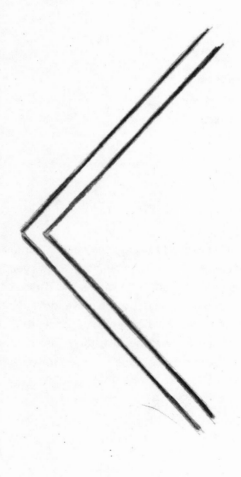

KENAZ

remembering
more than blood
my ancestors
were etched inside
Kenaz
split me open
I penetrated the darkness
I saw what was destroyed
spun and woven
frayed and worn
the strands of Wyrd
retied

What do you know inside your bones, in the heart of your very
being, that you did not study or learn? We all carry ancestral
wisdom and memories. Kenaz reminds us that we do not need
light to see in the dark. The necessity of light is relevant only
when using our literal eyes. Like a wedge, the power of this
rune splits us open so we can see what we already know.
Find your way back by following the threads of Wyrd. Kenaz
whispers to you the secrets of who you are and where you
come from. Is your ancestral wisdom calling you home so you
can retie and reweave your threads?

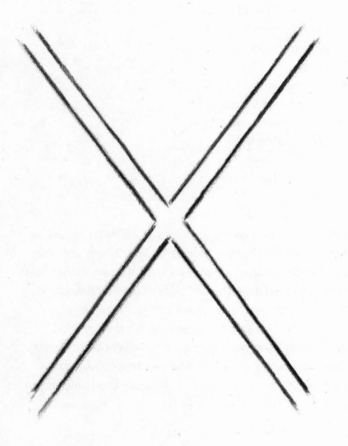

GEBO

Gebo
all gifts and obligations
carry your presence
the runes
the gods
demand of me
a sacrifice
what I pledge
binds me
releases me
all gain requires loss
all life is equal exchange

Life is the gift of equal exchange. Of energies, of obligations, contracts and agreements. It is not possible to give if there is no receiver. Gebo reminds us to pay attention to what we accept, making sure we have integrity around what is expected of us in the exchange. Gebo also demands of us integrity when we are the giver. Do we give freely or are there hooks of expectation hidden in the gifts? Are we held hostage by the stories we create around the gifts we are given? Gifts involve loss as well as gain. Do you honor your contracts and agreements? Do you bind yourself in word without considering the consequences?

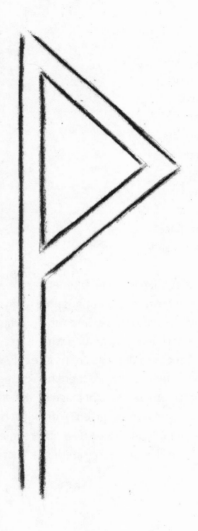

WUNJO

Wunjo
fulfiller of wishes
you care not
for wisdom or folly
you lead me
both to joy
and madness
in death
in the presence of the gods
in sun filled halls
I drink

There is joy in community and there are obligations and responsibilities. This is the gentle breeze that causes the flag to flutter. Wunjo reminds us that even the slightest breeze can change the weather. The halls of death are filled with joy. The sun shines there when it is not present in the night sky. Who can judge the source of joy or the manner in which we find it or express it? What is the difference between joy and madness? Do you judge the methods or the substances used by others to obtain joy? Do you judge yourself? What are the differences that exist between joy, madness and ecstasy? How are they the same?

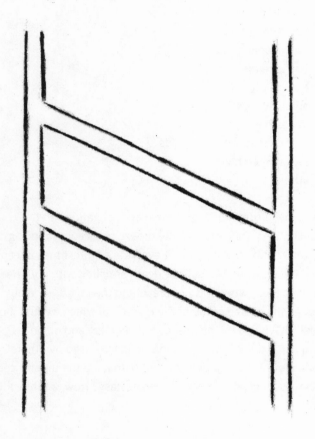

HAGALAZ

most holy of runes
fearsome stormbringer
the gods provided
signs and portents
greater than the realm of man
I ignored the warnings
bound in Helheim
by Hagalaz
Hela
braids and unbraids
my hair

Hagalaz is hard hitting, fast moving like a hailstorm. The energy of water quickly coming into crystal form. You are warned. Take shelter away from the storm. Its association with weather binds it together with the inevitable embrace of Hela, she who openly welcomes all of us in death. Pay attention. The storm is always the chaos. There is no way to control it or keep it from happening and yet it is from out of the storm that something new emerges. Hagalaz, the hailstorm with thunder and lightning, is tied to the storms of Thurisaz in a fertile, destructive way. Where are you bound because you did not heed the warnings?

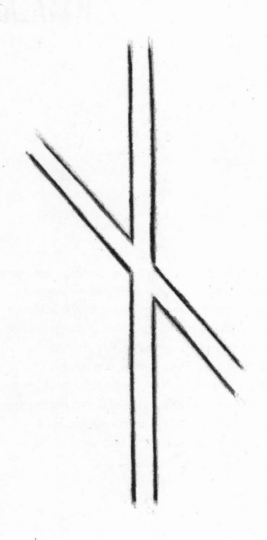

NAUTHIZ

summoned by need
gaunt from starvation
I emerge
slowly from the cave
Nauthiz
you are a hungry rune
fueled by bitter necessity
fierce with determination
your friction
sparks ancestral memory
ancient fires ignite

Not everything in life flows easily. We should not expect it to. Nauthiz reminds us that friction and resistance are necessary and necessity drives determination. You cannot start a fire unless things heat up. The necessity demands persistence. The wisdom to know how to do something exists in the need. You can only learn to do something by doing it. The bird knows how to peck its way out of the egg and it needs to peck in order to get out. And it takes effort. Our hunger for remembering the voice of our Mother Tongue is the need that calls us forth from the cave of forgetting. This awakens the ancestors so they can feed us. Just because something is challenging, difficult or requires effort is not an indication that it is not meant to be. Some things flow with ease. Others require friction.

ISA

Isa
realm of ice
home to all the runes
the crushing weight of ages
you float
hissing
groaning
there is movement
in your stillness
preservation in destruction
enthralled or released
I serve you

Isa is the beauty and danger of ice. It is the slowing down of the
movement of water that creates bridges. It imprisons as well as
preserves. It crushes and it floats. Within the singularity of Isa
all the runes are held, layered line by line, telling the stories
of the ages as does a glacier. We are in service to the constant
thaw and freeze of Isa. Movement is always present in stillness.
Ice enchants and enthralls. It holds us tight and causes us to
fall. Is there something in your life that has been frozen so
long it has become desiccated? Do you need to call upon Isa
to create a bridge so you can cross over something or move to
the other side? Are you floating on the surface or are you being
crushed?

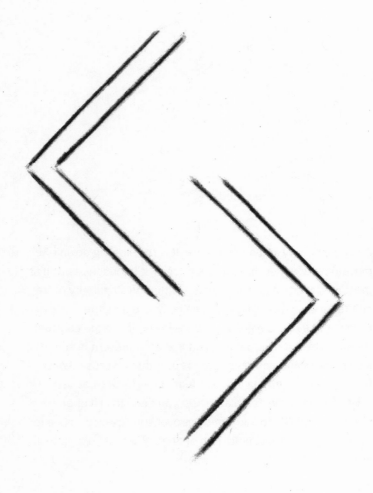

JERA

the wheel turns
Jera reaps
threshes
the golden hair of Sif
I must learn
to rest and labor
with the seasons
I cannot rush
I cannot delay
life
comes from death
at harvest

The great wheel turns. It is time to harvest that which has ripened or gone to seed. When something ends, something new begins. Life comes from death, always. When you live in harmony with the rhythm of nature you understand that life cannot be rushed nor can it be delayed. You can perhaps control what you plant but you cannot control the outcome. Acorns can only grow into oak trees. Cloudberries do not grow in the desert. Discernment is necessary when we make decisions regarding survival and Jera asks us to consider if we have made the right choices about what we gather in and what we leave behind in the fields.

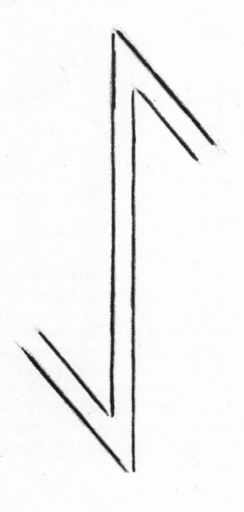

EIHWAZ

I come to see
Eihwaz
sacred yew of life
growing
from death
singing
songs of renewal
who will I become
through willing sacrifice
self to self
fearing the end
I forget to live

The cycle of life and death is present in all runes. Eihwaz resides in the yew tree, the branches growing up and then down. Even though the center appears to be dead eventually it sends up new life. We must seek out the roots in the dark places of wisdom in order to grow. Are you afraid of death? Then you have forgotten how to live. Do you turn away or pretend that it will not happen? If we are consumers then we must know that we too shall be consumed. What in your life needs to be offered up so something new can grow out of the middle?

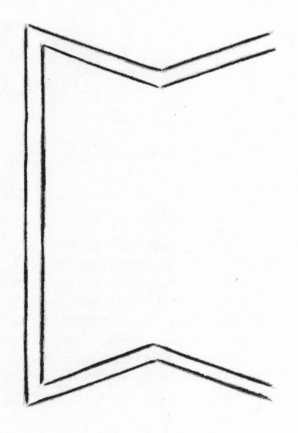

PERTHO

Pertho
you are the pouch
guarded
by the Norns
a womb holding secrets
a woman
crouching
in childbirth
the gods demand both
play and sacrifice
taking me down
to the roots and well

How comfortable are you with uncertainty? You cannot play
the game unless you are willing to take a chance. The pouch
is open, ready for you to reach in and take hold of some of its
contents. The Nornir know all that Pertho holds. They are the
pouch and they are the contents. The mother gives birth to
what is already inside, the unknown known. We can be pious
and overly concerned with what we deem as spiritual but the
gods demand that we are willing to play the game as well. Roll
the dice.

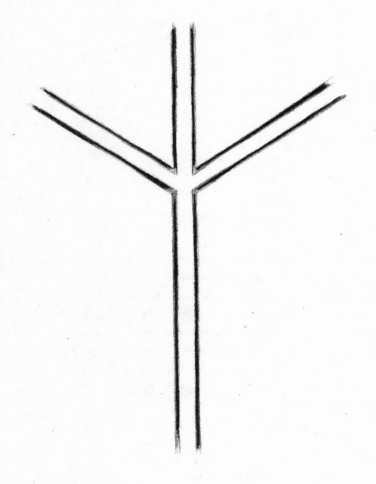

ALᚴIZ

Algiz
of the antlers
tine before the eyes
embodied
in my upraised arms
I ask
am I the hunter or the hunted
in danger and protected
I follow the herds
across the ice

Algiz protects the antlered, reindeer grandmother as she leads
the herd to food and a safe place to give birth. Hiding has
two sides, danger and protection. You must decide if you are
the hunter or the hunted. Take a stance and reveal yourself,
in all the glory of who you are. It is dangerous to cross the ice
yet you will surely starve if you do not. It is often said that
Algiz belongs to the elk or the moose. It is much more likely it
belongs to the reindeer. Both the female and the male wear the
antlers.

SOWELO

I rise at dawn
to greet you Sunna
singing your song
Sowelo
you grant sight
you blind the arrogant
wolf chased
horse drawn
you disappear
again
I rise at dawn
to greet you

Sowelo will lead you to Sunna, the sun, and she will tell you
where you are and what time it is. Sowelo is the light that is
necessary for warmth and growth. But beware. Do you take
the sun for granted? She allows us to see with our eyes and
she blinds us as well if we try to gaze upon her face. We must
celebrate her return as well as her departure. Sowelo creates
the great sun wheel with her body, turning and returning.
Sowelo can be flashes of light. Lightning bolts that suddenly
illuminate the darkness. Do you rise at dawn to greet the sun?
Have you ever greeted the night? She too rises up out of earth.

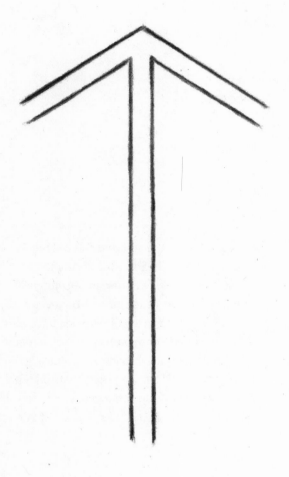

TEIWAZ

can there be justice
in lies
I ask of Tyr
order over chaos
is loss always present
in compromise
strength of convictions
demands a price
who dares deny
the wolf
his true nature

Teiwaz is the arrow that pierces you when you are off course,
out of alignment, lacking integrity and honor. It is the sacred
pole pointing north, Frigga's spindle around which the heavens
spin. How much of yourself has been eaten away because
you are not telling the truth about your life to yourself and to
others? Loss is always present when we compromise. When we
withhold what is true we set in motion the loss of something
that can never be regained. Where in your life have you settled
for less because you were afraid to tell the truth?

BERKANA

I am warned
the devouring mother
discards as well as nurtures
she who births
also destroys
when I poison you
Berkana
you feed me
death in return
beware
this is the mystery
life

Berkana protects us with the wisdom of the mother. She
reminds us that we must take care of ourselves first so we have
something to give to others. Berkana knows when to nurture
and nourish and when to push away something that is not
viable. She also knows when she must eat her own young.
The law of life is also the mystery. This rune of the mother is
in perfect alignment with the giantess Jord who is the earth,
especially now that she is taking care of herself by causing
great upheaval. Is she perhaps eating her young? Is she feeding
us death in exchange for the poison we have heaped upon
her? She consumes everything eventually so it can be reused.
Are you being poisoned or are you perhaps the one doing the
poisoning? Where in your life do you allow others to feed off
of you at your own expense? Are you still breast feeding your
teenagers or perhaps even your partner?

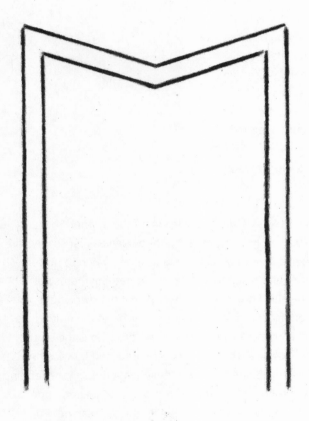

EHWAZ

sacred horse
saddled
you carry the gods
to their greatness
the dangler knows
rhythm and movement
mastery and surrender
riding your energies
Ehwaz
I set boundaries
while crossing them
I become my equal

You cannot ride a horse by pulling back on the reins. Nor can you drive a car with one foot on the gas pedal and the other on the brake. Ehwaz is about movement that is in alignment with and equal to itself. Ask Ehwaz to show you where you are involved with someone or something that is not in alignment with who you are. Ask Ehwaz to show you where you are dragging someone who is not pulling their own weight. Are you a draft horse harnessed to a Shetland pony, trying to pull a wagon to market? It will not work. You will only go in circles. This rune vibrates with the truth that you cannot master anything unless you are willing to surrender to it. Is there a place in your life where you need to travel alone?

MANNAZ

all the holy races
stand connected
at the bridge
where have I separated joy
my sex
from the gods
my body
from the divine
Ask and Embla
join together
Mannaz
breathes as one

There is no separation between humanity and divinity. We
emerge from the same place, the chaos and darkness of the
Void. We all come from the same mother. We are whole and
complete, lacking nothing. There is nothing wrong or sinful or
defective about our human bodies. There is a doubling of joy
when we celebrate and honor ourselves as divine. Mannaz
invites you to explore your beliefs and feelings about your
body, your sexuality and your kinship with the gods.

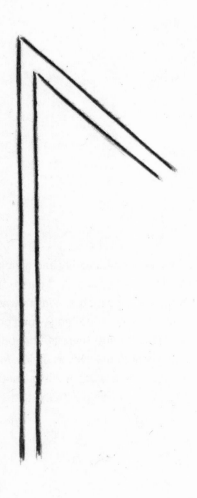

LAGUZ

you are lake and well
stream and fen
the waters of my own body
shape shifting
Laguz
deceptive
destructive
life giving
I dare not judge
all rivers flow
the ocean refuses no one

Water is both life giving and death dealing. Laguz is all waters of the earth, both inside and outside our bodies. Water flows and its nature is to meander. We cannot run out of water. It is part of a closed system of endless return. It dissolves things, moves things and erodes the land as it builds land. The waters of your body are in rhythm with the cycles of the moon and sea. Laguz is the fluid movement of the waters of our emotions. We dare not judge what we feel as being bad or good. We must allow for the feelings to be.

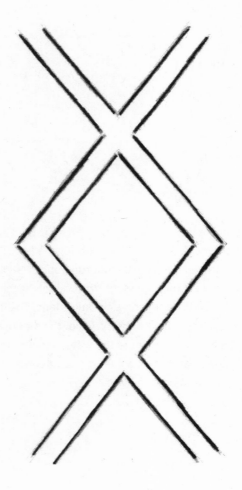

INGWAZ

fully aroused by her mound
the honored doorway
the sacred
mystery of stored seed
bursts forth
blessing the mother
brother sister lover
with gifts
ancestor to kings
Ingwaz
engorged
I follow your wagon

Ingwaz is a sexual rune, the fertile potential that holds all possibility. Freya and Freyr are twins, sister and brother. They are both aroused and engorged and their fertility is a blessing for the land and all who dwell therein. Do you honor the power of your own body's creative potential or do you shut it down? Do you recognize your ability to create as a gift that connects to your sexuality as well as your spirituality? Ingwaz is the strand of DNA that carries the memories of who we are. It can be twisted open or closed. Ingwaz often appears to remind you of what is possible, what is held within the womb of all potential.

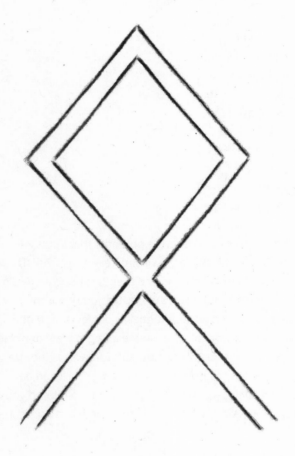

◊THILA

Othila
I carry you
in my body
you have fed me
the bones of my ancestors
unto you
I offer up the blood legacy
for future generations
held in the memory of Mimir

Othila is the sacred enclosure of your ancestral land. Where
were your ancestors born? Where are they buried? Their bodies
feed the earth and the earth feeds your body. Will you honor
your ancestors by remembering who you are? Are you willing
to offer yourself up so the future can be remembered? Do you
go to the waters of the Wells to connect with the wisdom of
the dark and the Nornir? Othila is a rune about life and it is a
rune about death. In order for you to inherit anything from your
ancestors, someone must die.

DAGAZ

arms folded
I cross myself
the still point
constantly moving
leaving
returning
emerging
from light darkness
where they meet
am I willing
to be nothing
Dagaz the double edge
brings death and birth

Dagaz is daybreak and nightfall, the extremes of the solstices
on each end and the threshold place of the equinox in the
center. It is the transformation inherent in metamorphosis
present in the butterfly and the caterpillar. It is the double edge
of leaving and returning, of killing on the battlefield and cutting
the umbilical cord at birth. Dagaz asks you if you are willing
to be nothing in the middle. This rune brings us to balance,
reminding us that daybreak is equal to nightfall. Are you willing
to be both?

Nothing I say is true.

Everything I say is true.

The truth lives in the questions.

5

GUIDED
MEDITATIONS

CENTER MEDITATION

Before you begin this guided meditation, find a place where you feel safe and comfortable, a place where you can fully relax without being interrupted or disturbed.
The intention is to relax without falling asleep.
You may want to have a notebook or journal close by so you can write about your experience after the meditation.

The Center

When you feel safe and comfortable, close your eyes and take a long, slow, deep breath. And then slowly exhale. And another long, slow, deep breath and then exhale. Continue your slow, even breathing, in and out, in and out, as you relax into your body.

Imagine if you can that you have been walking along a lovely path, enjoying life, listening to bird song and smelling the sweet fragrance of the flowers.
As you walk, you come upon an enormous forest filled with every species of tree imaginable, trees from all climates and all parts of the world. You stand in awe at the edge of the forest and you wonder how this is possible, how all these trees can be growing together in the same place. You wonder and yet you realize that the answer does not matter.
You stand there peering in among all the trees, looking for your tree, and finally you see it. This particular tree has always held a special meaning for you. Its bark and branches, leaves and limbs are familiar. This is your tree, your favorite tree, growing here among all the other trees of the world.

Slowly you enter the forest, walking toward your tree. You reach out and lovingly touch its bark. You thank it for being so strong and beautiful, so deeply rooted and so gloriously open. You stand in its presence and you embrace it, wrapping your arms around its trunk as far as you can reach. You stay with this feeling, experiencing your life force flowing with the spirit of the tree. And as you continue to breathe you realize that you have become one with it, its roots, its branches, its trunk.

At the same time you know you have merged with the great tree, the World Tree, the tree that grows in the Center of the Wheel. You are connected to the Center of the universe, the silent, still place from which all life emerges and where all life returns and where all life begins again.

And you breathe in this great wisdom.

After a while you notice some movement and your attention is turned toward a squirrel who is running up and down the trunk of the Great Tree, top to bottom, branches to roots, back and forth, up and down.

This is Ratatoskr, the famed squirrel of Norse legend. Its role it is to carry messages back and forth between the eagle and the falcon who dwell in the highest branches in the top of the World Tree and the great dragon serpent Nidhogg who dwells below forever gnawing on the roots.

Suddenly the squirrel stops, as if waiting for you to speak. And so you ask it,

Tell me if you will, what messages do you carry back and forth, from the branches to the roots and back again? Do these messages hold any wisdom for me? I have merged with the World Tree, and you are now scurrying up and down my trunk.

You listen to what the squirrel has to tell you. And when it has finished you thank it. And you know you will remember all that you need to remember for its message is new and its message is as old as time.

You continue to listen until you begin to notice your breath and you slowly take your arms from around the tree and you step back, first looking at the tree, thanking it for being there, and then gazing around the forest, thanking all the trees.

You turn and begin to find your way back to the path.

You take a long, deep breath that brings you back into your body and into the preset moment.

You open your eyes slowly and close them.

You open your eyes slowly and close them.

You open your eyes and then keep them open with a soft gaze until you are ready.

EAST MEDITATION

Before you begin this guided meditation, find a place where
you feel safe and comfortable, a place where you can fully relax
without being interrupted or disturbed.
The intention is to relax without falling asleep.
You may want to have a notebook or journal close by so you
can write about your experience after the meditation.

The East

When you feel safe and comfortable close your eyes and take
a long, slow, deep breath. And then slowly exhale. And another
long, slow, deep breath and then exhale. Continue your slow,
even breathing, in and out, in and out, as you relax into your body.

Imagine that it is very early in the morning, that dark time just
before dawn. It is cold and there is dew on the ground from
the night. You silently slip out of bed, wrapping yourself up in
a still-warm blanket and barefooted, you step outside. As your
feet touch the path, you are startled by how cold the ground
is. Quietly you walk, winding your way up to the top of the hill
just to the east of your home. You stand motionless, bundled
against the chill of the dawn, silently waiting for the return
of the sun, trusting that she will once again reward you with
another day.
As you stand atop the hill you allow your thoughts to wander.
As you do this, you hear the undersong of the universe, the
melody that weaves together all that is.
As you listen to this melody you realize that it connects with
your heart, the place where you keep your longings, your

yearnings and your dreams. At times you have pushed these dreams away or tried to ignore them because somehow you do not believe that it is possible for you to follow your heart or satisfy your longings.

As the sun begins to rise, you feel her gentle warmth on your face.

You feel yourself step into the Center, carrying with you your dreams.

You connect with the Tree, she who guards and listens. You ask her to share her wisdom.

You ask the Tree,

What is the root of my longing?
How expansive and far reaching can it be?

You ask the Tree to teach you how to fully live in harmony with your heart's desire.

And you travel up and down the trunk of the Tree, above and below, above and below, and you listen.

You have been on the hill a long time and you begin to realize that the sun has fully risen above the horizon. She is bright and warm.

You gather up, into your heart, all that you have been shown by the Tree.

You turn and step back onto the path and slowly make your way down the hill, back to your home, to the present moment.

You take a deep breath, coming back into your body, and you slowly open your eyes.

And you remember.

SOUTH MEDITATION

Before you begin this guided meditation, find a place where you feel safe and comfortable, a place where you can fully relax without being interrupted or disturbed.
The intention is to relax without falling asleep.
You may want to have a notebook or journal close by so you can write about your experience after the meditation.

The South

When you feel safe and comfortable close your eyes and take a long, slow, deep breath. And then slowly exhale. And another long, slow, deep breath and then exhale. Continue your slow, even breathing, in and out, in and out, as you relax into your body.

Imagine that it is a warm, lazy, summer day. You find yourself sitting in the shade of an ancient, gnarled tree that is deeply rooted in the countryside. You are comfortable in the presence of this well-loved friend. You seek solitude here away from the noise and busyness of the city. You visit often. You can smell the warm earth, the wild flowers and the fields of hay. With your eyes closed you listen to the buzzing of bees. Your mind begins to wander back and forth across the landscape of your life and you pause in different places recalling times when you were patient and times when you were not, times when you were still and quiet, at rest, and times when you felt hurried, rushed or impatient. And as you remember all of this you come upon a place where you stop and linger.

You know deep inside yourself that this is a place where you need to root and ground so you can stabilize and grow.

You know deep inside yourself that you must be still so something can ripen and mature. You focus awhile on these things.

You are silent. You are patient.

You linger in the places of rooting and maturing.

You linger in the places of unfolding and allowing.

You are relaxed in your body in the present moment.

You thank the tree for her shade.

You thank the earth for her support.

You begin again to pay attention to your breath.

In and out. In and out. In and out.

When you are ready you slowly open your eyes and then close them. Open your eyes and then close them.

Take a deep breath and find yourself back in the present moment.

WEST MEDITATION

Before you begin this guided meditation, find a place where you feel safe and comfortable, a place where you can fully relax without being interrupted or disturbed.
The intention is to relax without falling asleep.
You may want to have a notebook or journal close by so you can write about your experience after the meditation.

The West

When you feel safe and comfortable close your eyes and take a long, slow, deep breath. And then slowly exhale. And another long, slow, deep breath and then exhale. Continue your slow, even breathing, in and out, in and out, as you relax into your body.

Imagine that it is evening and you have gone to the beach with the intention of watching the sun set into the ocean. As you gaze out across the waves you can see the glowing, orange ball of the sun as it slowly begins to disappear into the water. A slight breeze comes up and you wrap yourself in a blanket as you feel a bit of a chill. It is sunset, the ending of another day and the beginning of a new one. The night is rising up behind you. The stars are beginning to twinkle in the sky.
As the sun sets your mind wanders and drifts remembering the things you have learned so far from the runes and the wisdom of the lost teachings.
Life. It is about constant change.
You reflect upon your life, recalling things you have planted and begun, things you have nurtured and cared for, things you have let go of and things you have set aside.

You reflect upon the time you have spent watching things mature and ripen and as you watch the sun set into the ocean you reflect upon things in your life right now that have come to maturity, ripened and grown to fullness.

This is the time of discernment.

What in your life needs to be gathered in or harvested?

What needs to be left alone, allowed to fall from the tree?

What needs to be left in the fields to wilt and rot and be given back to the earth?

What do you need to gather in and store away for the coming winter?

What do you need to save in order to plant again in spring?

How much do you dare to eat when nothing is growing?

As you continue to wander your way around and through these questions, wrapped in your blanket, the sun finally and completely disappears into the sea.

She is gone now and only an afterglow remains.

You sit and wait and reflect until the blanket of night completely covers the sky.

You wrap your own blanket more tightly around your body.

Slowly you wander your way back along the beach toward home. With each slow step you are more confident in the decisions you have made and the actions you are going to take.

As you continue walking you begin once again to pay attention to your breath.

In and out. In and out. In and out.

You take one long, slow, deep breath. You open your eyes and then close them. You open your eyes and then close them. You open your eyes and leave them open with a soft gaze.

You have walked your way back home.

You take one deep breath that brings you back, fully present in your body.

NORTH MEDITATION

Before you begin this guided meditation, find a place where
you feel safe and comfortable, a place where you can fully relax
without being interrupted or disturbed.
The intention is to be able to fully relax without falling asleep.
You may want to have a notebook or journal close by so you
can write about your experience after the meditation.

The North

When you feel safe and comfortable please begin by closing
your eyes and taking a long, slow, deep breath. And then slowly
exhale. And another long, slow, deep breath and then exhale.
Continue your slow, even breathing, in and out, in and out, as
you relax into your body.

Imagine if you can that it is Winter Solstice and the rising sun
has just aligned perfectly with the long passage that leads
into the depths of the ancient cairn. The beam of light shines
brightly on the triple spiral carved on the sacred stone. This
is the mystery and the miracle. The sun at Winter Solstice. It
returns. It happened this morning just as it has happened every
year for as long as time can be remembered.
It is bitter cold. You shiver even though you are warmly dressed.
You tremble with excitement. This is the year that has been
chosen for you to enter into the womb of the sacred mound
and bring your offering to the altar.
You have been preparing for this special occasion since
childhood and you patiently waited each year, wondering when
it would be your time.

You have carried in your heart the question of your offering.
What will it be?
What will you bring to place upon the altar?
When the day dawned this morning, you realized that you
knew what the offering would be. It had come to you during the
longest night of the year.
You slowly enter the mouth of the womb-like cairn, carrying in
your arms, under your woolen cloak and close to your heart, the
offering.
Torches and candles light the long passageway you must walk.
At the end you reach a large chamber and as you step into the
space you see there are many who have gathered inside to
greet you, each one holding a candle.
You approach the altar in the center.
You clutch your bundle to your breast.
You take a breath and then you lovingly and willingly place
your offering upon the stone. You quietly sing the old songs as
you gently unwrap your gift. You take one last look and touch
it with your fingertips. You turn and walk silently to the place
where the sacred fire burns and you touch your finger to the
ash and soot and then mark the sign of Gebo, the gift
of sacrifice, on your forehead.
It is complete. It is finished.
It is now time for you to pass through the gates, to step across
the threshold, into this next part of your life. You walk down
the passage, back the way you came in, proudly wearing the
mark of Gebo, knowing you are the same and knowing you are
different.

As you step through the low arch of the passage, out into the open, you take a long, deep breath.
You are coming back into your body, back into the present moment.
You slowly open your eyes and close them.
Slowly open your eyes and close them.
Slowly open your eyes and when you feel ready, leave them open with a soft gaze.

Sometimes all that needs to change
are the meanings we attach
to the stories we tell.